Cash
Flow
Forecasting

Cash Flow Forecasting

William Loscalzo, MBA, CPA

PRENTICE HALL
BUSINESS & PROFESSIONAL DIVISION
A division of Simon & Schuster
Englewood Cliffs, New Jersey 07632

Prentice-Hall International, Inc. *London*
Prentice-Hall of Australia, Pty. Ltd., *Sydney*
Prentice-Hall of Canada, Inc., *Toronto*
Prentice-Hall of India Private Ltd., *New Delhi*
Prentice-Hall of Japan, Inc. *Tokyo*
Prentice-Hall of Southeast Asia Pte., Ltd., *Singapore*
Whitehall Books, Ltd., *Wellington, New Zealand*
Editora Prentice-Hall do Brasil Ltda., *Rio de Janeiro*
Prentice-Hall Hispanoamericana, S.A., *Mexico*

10   9   8   7   6

Library of Congress Cataloging in Publication Data

Loscalzo, William.
  Cash flow forecasting.

  Includes index.
  1. Cash flow—Forecasting.   2. Cash management.
I. Title.
HG4028.C45L68   658.1′5244   81-20934
                                       AACR2

ISBN 0-13-116013-3

PRENTICE HALL
BUSINESS & PROFESSIONAL DIVISION
A division of Simon & Schuster
Englewood Cliffs, New Jersey 07632

PRINTED IN THE UNITED STATES OF AMERICA

Contents

Preface

For many people, the transition from public accounting to industry can be unexpectedly difficult. Likewise, students making a transition to the business world will find that it is very different from the business school environment. All too often people realize that their academic backgrounds and possibly their public accounting experience have not fully prepared them to deal with the real-world problems of business. This is especially true in the area of forecasting cash flow. Those who are just beginning a career in the financial area of a corporation may very well know how to classify accounts and draft financial statements in accordance with generally accepted accounting principles (GAAP). But very often, they have no experience in how to go about preparing a forecast. In fact, they may not even know what assumptions are necessary and how to obtain them.

Cash Flow Forecasting is designed to help ease the transition from academia or public accounting to the real world of business. Cash flow forecasts are a way of life in the corporate business environment. Day-to-day decisions and long-range plans must be based on accurate forecasts of cash flow projections under varying assumptions.

This book is designed for controllers, treasurers, and other financial people, as well as accountants, managers, and students who want a practical rather than theoretical grasp of cash flow forecasting. This "hands-on" approach to cash flow forecasting will provide the reader with an in-depth review of key forecasting areas such as sales, money market instruments, and debt. Using a hypothetical case study and easy-to-follow worksheets and statements, you will learn:

- What areas need to be forecasted
- What forecast assumptions are required
- Where to obtain forecast assumptions
- How to prepare detailed cash forecast calculations
- What shortcuts can be taken in preparing detailed calculations
- How to prepare forecast worksheets
- How to present a cash flow forecast
- How to adjust a forecast on the basis of a series of "what if" questions
- How to work with several different formats for cash flow forecasts

William Loscalzo

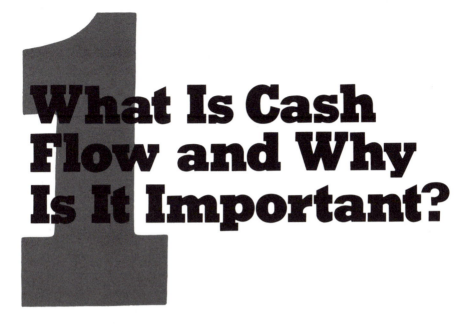

CHAPTER

What Is Cash Flow and Why Is It Important?

On September 30, 1979, my company, Security Mortgage Investors (SMI), reported net income for the year of $2,206,000, after having accumulated five consécutive years of losses totaling $25,730,000. Not only has SMI continued to show earnings but it is now in the process of acquiring a savings and loan association with a net worth of almost $11 million. Why then are some companies forced into bankruptcy after accumulating only $2 or $3 million of losses while other companies with large losses, like SMI, turn around and begin to expand? The answer is simple. Companies go bankrupt because they cannot pay their bills, not because they have accumulated losses. SMI, for example, was able to generate cash through the sale and payoff of assets despite operating losses.

Earnings versus Cash Flow

Earnings and cash flow are two entirely different concepts. *Earnings* is an accounting concept created by accounting convention, statements of the American Institute of Certified Public Accountants and the Financial Accounting Standards Board, and regulations promulgated by the Securities and Exchange Commission. *Cash flow*, on the other hand, is based on the timing of the receipts and disbursements of cash. Although most shareholders claim they are concerned with earnings, they are really only interested in dividends that will be distributed to them and in the ultimate cash value of their investments. A prime example of this philosophy is

1

public tax-shelter real estate partnerships. On December 31, 1976, SB Partners reported accumulated losses totaling $11,740,731. In spite of these losses, the selling price rose steadily from an initial offering price of $10,000 per unit to $13,800 per unit. A tax-shelter investment will lose money on paper for tax purposes but will not require additional outlays of funds and will not erode the initial investment. Although SB Partners "lost" money during the period, real estate values rose, thus protecting the cash value of the initial investment.

Another example of the confusion between earnings and cash flow was recently illustrated at a graduate business-games session at a New York City university. Several groups of students had formed "corporations" and had prepared cash flow projections to accompany their hypothetical loan applications. Each and every student had defined operating cash flow as net income plus depreciation or net income exclusive of depreciation. A review of the following items will point out why this income-statement approach is incorrect.

Depreciation. The most obvious difference between earnings and cash flow, depreciation is merely the accounting convention of allocating the cost of an asset over its *useful life*. This is a somewhat arbitrary period of time which, pursuant to accounting regulations, cannot exceed 40 years.

Amortization. This, too, is an accounting convention that allocates costs over an arbitrary time period.

Prepaid Items. These items are cash payments made in one period that reduce earnings in future periods, not in the period of payment. Typically, insurance, supplies, maintenance contracts, etc., are paid in advance but are charged to earnings in the subsequent period.

Sales/Accounts Receivable. Accrual basis accounting allows noncash sales to be recorded when title passes. Cash flow, however, is affected only when the receivable is paid.

Inventory. The matching concept requires inventory to be charged to cost of goods sold (which reduces earnings) when a sale takes place. However, most inventory is paid long before its related sale is made.

Constant Payments on Interest-Bearing Obligations. Most intermediate- or long-term interest-bearing receivables and payables require monthly payments of principal and interest until the obligation is paid in full. Only the interest portion of this payment is reflected in earnings, while cash flow is affected by both principal and interest.

Property, Plant, and Equipment. Cash is reduced by both the initial down payment and all subsequent installment payments. Earnings, on the other hand, is affected only by depreciation. Since land is never depreciated, earnings is never affected by its cost.

Statement of Changes Approach to Cash Flow Forecasting

Many individuals turn to the statement of changes in financial position as a starting point for cash flow projections. Like the income statement, this statement is the result of accounting convention and bears little resemblance to actual cash flow. To illustrate this difference, consider a statement of changes in financial position prepared in the working capital format. The cash purchase of inventory will not affect working capital (current assets less current liabilities) since the increase in a short-term asset (inventory) is offset by the decrease of a short-term asset (cash). However, by definition, cash is affected. Conversely, the extension of a short- to a long-term obligation affects working capital but does not have an effect on cash.

Even a statement of changes in financial position using the cash format is misleading. A company may show no change in cash because all excess cash was invested in marketable securities. However, this company has significantly improved its cash flow position despite the fact that the cash balance remains unchanged.

Importance of Cash Flow

Let's now deal with the question of why cash flow is so important. In essence, cash flow is the lifeblood of a company and is fundamental to its very existence. It indicates whether or not a company can pay its bills.

If cash flow were a steady stream of receipts and disbursements, forecasting would be unnecessary. Under such conditions, if all bills were paid last month, they again would be paid this month, and so on. However, in reality, cash flow fluctuates from day to day, month to month, season to season. The following items are just a few factors that contribute to the ups and downs of cash flow:

- Some months have five weekly payrolls, while other months have only four.
- Raw materials purchased in bulk often have significant discounts. A company may permit its inventory to decline until the appropriate economic order quantity may be purchased.
- Sales are often seasonal. Consequently, payments will fluctuate.
- Debt payments may be on a semiannual basis, an annual basis, etc.
- New property, plant, equipment, and leasehold improvements are not purchased evenly throughout the year.
- Commissions or bonuses may be paid annually but accrued for throughout the year.
- Factories are often shut down for repairs or vacations.

The timing of some of the above factors may be optional and within management's control. For example, payments of inventory or the purchase of leasehold improvements a week late rarely has a devastating effect on a company. On the other hand, the nonpayment of a bank loan or required debenture sinking fund payment may cause a default and subsequent involuntary bankruptcy. Therefore, the ability to determine—to forecast—these peak cash flow demands becomes vital to corporate management.

Accurate cash forecasting can also prevent the loss of earnings to a company. It can be quite embarrassing and costly for a new cash manager to secure a high-yielding 60-day money market instrument only to discover a week later that cash is needed to purchase inventory and the security must be sold at a loss.

Types of Forecasts

There are many different types of forecasts, each serving a separate and distinct purpose. The following are just a few types of forecasts and their related uses.

Short-Term. Usually covering a period of less than one year, this type of forecast is designed to assist in the day-to-day operations of the business. It principally highlights the peaks and valleys resulting from seasonal sales, inventory purchases, etc.

Intermediate-Term. Usually covering one to three years, this type of forecast is principally used to evaluate the company's ability or inability to meet a specific cash requirement, for example, a debenture payment or the estimated payback period on an investment.

Long-Term. Usually covering in excess of three years, this type of forecast is used almost exclusively for long-range planning for acquisitions, expansions, etc.

Since forecasts are strictly management tools, they must be sensitive to management's needs. Therefore, each of the above types of forecasts, especially the intermediate- and long-term forecasts, is often further subdivided into the following classifications.

Worst Case. This forecast is prepared using the most *conservative* assumptions; for example, the highest expected interest rates on debt, a low sales growth, or, even worse, no sales growth. It is often used by management to determine the lowest return a company can accept on an investment or the most a company can borrow and ensure repayment.

Best Case. This forecast is prepared using the most aggressive assumptions, for example, the lowest interest rates on debt, the maximum growth rate, etc. It is often used to determine the amount of growth that can be obtained before new equipment must be purchased or new financing must be obtained, etc.

"As Is." This forecast is prepared using the most likely assumptions, for example, continued sales level, no expansion, etc. It is usually prepared to assist management in planning for the everyday needs of the business.

Forecast Flexibility

Even the above classifications are not sacrosanct. The most important attribute of a forecast is its flexibility. It is through its flexibility that a forecast can best assist management as a planning tool. Since this flexibility is so important, Chapter 9 will explain how to structure a forecast to answer a series of "what if" questions. For example, suppose management has decided to buy out a competitor to achieve a greater share of the market, to eliminate competition, and to raise prices. A *long-term, "as is"* forecast might be prepared using anticipated cash flow from operations and existing bank lines. Such a forecast may indicate that the company is short the required cash for the acquisition. Management might then ask, *what if* the company disposes of factory X to finance the transaction? It is not enough to factor the anticipated sales price of factory X in the cash flow. The loss of sales due to factory X's not being in operation, the increased interest expense on borrowings to finance the acquisition, and the cash flow expected from the acquired company must also be considered.

Management might further wish to see a *long-term, worst case* forecast in order to quantify its maximum business risk if the company is acquired. For example, if interest rates rise and collections taper off, will there be enough cash flow to fund start-up operations at the new company? Or management might want a *long-term, best case* forecast in order to entice bankers to fund the purchase price of the forecast.

In reality, management will probably ask for all of the above forecasts before making the final decisions on acquiring the company. This does not mean that there is one right or wrong forecast. Rather, each forecast serves a purpose. Each is a projection of the expected results of a given set of assumptions. A list of all assumptions used should be prepared and should accompany any forecast presentation.

Format of This Book

This book is designed to show you how to prepare a forecast. Each chapter will develop a step-by-step, area-by-area forecast of the MBL Manufacturing Company. Whether you are dealing with a manufacturing company, a bank, a finance company, or a retail chain store, the principles of forecasting are the same. For example: Is there any real difference between a manufacturing company with investments in marketable securities and a bank with its investment portfolio? If you know how to forecast a mortgage payable on a factory, you can also forecast a mortgage receivable for a bank. After all, isn't the concept the same, with the numbers merely being on different sides of the balance sheet? Are the problems of forecasting inventory for a retail chain store very different from the problems of forecasting inventory for a manufacturing company? Isn't forecasting payroll for a steel mill operator the same as for a margin clerk in a brokerage house? If you can adjust a forecast for the purchase of a new factory, can't you also adjust a forecast for a new branch office of a bank? And what about size? The only real difference between a $100,-000,000 steel mill in Pittsburgh and a $100,000 weaving machine in the garment center in New York is 000s. With a little imagination, MBL Manufacturing Company could be Chase Manhattan Bank, Merrill Lynch, or General Motors, since the concepts are the same.

For the purposes of this book, let's assume tbat MBL's management has asked for a one-year cash flow forecast. However, for illustrative purposes, the forecast will also include some long-term activities. We will further assume that our forecast will be given to outside third parties such as banks, investment bankers, etc. Therefore, we will also prepare a forecasted balance sheet and income statement. These projected financial statements will show creditors that certain ratios and net worth tests are still being met.

Each chapter of this book will outline the assumptions you must make in order to forecast a particular area. In addition, the chapters will discuss the internal and/or external events or conditions that affect each assumption. The text will provide guidance on how to obtain each assumption. It will also walk you through the detailed calculations required to mathematically assemble the forecast. After the detailed calculations are made, formulas and shortcuts that will facilitate the actual preparation of the forecast will be reviewed. Worksheets at the end of each chapter summarize the forecast operations completed in that section.

After the complete forecast has been prepared, we will review in detail the types of "sensitivity" (i.e., "what if") items that management most frequently requires. Then we will examine several cash flow formats that can be adapted to meet management's needs.

Sales / Accounts Receivable

Sales, like many of the areas we will be discussing, do *not* directly affect cash. Only the ultimate realization of the cash receipt for a sale will affect the cash portion of our forecast. Despite the fact that a bona fide sale exists, title has been transferred, merchandise has been shipped, gains or losses have been recognized for accounting purposes, invoices have been sent, etc., there is absolutely no effect on the cash flow of a company until payment is received. This may seem obvious, but how many times have you tried to prepare a cash flow forecast beginning with the sales number from the income statement?

Sales Factors Affecting Cash

Before any attempt can be made at quantifying the cash effect of sales, it is necessary to determine the factors that influence the ultimate realization of cash. This will give us a base from which we can develop our forecasting model. One way to do this is to answer the following questions:

1. What is total sales volume?
2. What is total sales value?
3. What amount, if any, represents cash sales?
4. When is cash contractually due?

7

5. What amount of cash is collectible:
   a. Are there expected sales returns or allowances?
   b. Are amounts uncollectible due to outside external sources, i.e., bad debts?
6. What amount of cash is due:
   a. Are discounts available?
   b. Are such discounts taken?

The major portion of this chapter will be devoted to finding out where to get the answers to these questions and how to quantify them.

WHAT IS TOTAL SALES VOLUME?

Factors Affecting Sales Volume

Before beginning the actual forecasting of sales volume, a brief review of some of the internal and external factors affecting sales volume is essential.

Marketing Strategy. Sales are generated by sales personnel and promotion. Therefore, we should look at the size of the existing sales force, noting any increases or decreases in personnel. We should also discuss with management any anticipated increases or decreases in sales force size, any new advertising campaigns, and the expected impact of this advertising on sales.

New Product Lines. Determine if the company has recently marketed any new products and what the consumer response to these new products has been.

New Markets. Determine if the company has recently attempted to penetrate previously unsold markets and what the effect has been. As an example, Coca-Cola recently was the first American soft drink company to initiate sales in China.

Changes in Consumer Demand. If the consumer is to be the ultimate purchaser of our product, we must determine his or her desire to do so. For example, when gas lines grew and prices increased along with talk of gas rationing, sales of General Motor's Cadillacs declined while sales of subcompacts, especially small foreign cars, increased.

Competition. Since new entries into a field, new products, or increased marketing by an existing competitor all affect sales volume, we should determine their impact on sales. For example, airplanes have almost eliminated railroads in this country, and cassette tapes have replaced eight-track cartridges.

Availability of the Consumer Dollar. Sales are directly affected by the consumer's ability to purchase a product. As interest rates rise and construction costs increase, new housing starts will decline. Obviously, a company which caters to the construction industry will suffer reduced sales during such times. Conversely, in times of low interest and ready availability of funds, sales of items like recreational equipment flourish.

Each of the above factors will affect, to some extent, the sales volume being projected. Since the individual preparing the forecast rarely has the expertise to actually quantify the impact of these factors, he or she should at least be aware of the relationship these factors will have with sales. This awareness is also important in assessing the sales information provided by the person responsible for the sales function.

Forecasting Sales Volume

Let's see how we can project total sales volume for MBL. We have learned that the vice president and general sales manager, Mr. Williams, is responsible for all sales of the company. Our initial conversation with Mr. Williams revealed that current sales are approximately 2,000 units per month and that he is anticipating a 2% growth factor throughout the upcoming year.

One word of caution: The expectations of a sales manager rarely reflect reality and are usually quite optimistic. This optimism is not usually an intentional attempt to deceive but rather a difference in perspective. Sales people tend to view estimates and projections as targets to be obtained and, therefore, such goals are understandably high. Consequently, discussions with sales personnel should be prefaced by an outline of the objectives of the forecast, and its purpose; for example, is the forecast attempting to show a worst case or a best case scenario? What factors do we want considered in projecting growth? Specific guidelines should be set forth so that the projections are in tune with your understanding.

Before beginning the pencil pushing, sales information should be verified. A quick look at the month's sales orders, shipping reports, etc., would readily verify current sales. Next, we should verify the growth rate. It is not enough to merely verify past growth, since past growth may in no way relate to future growth. The company's sales force may have been increased, or new product lines may have been recently introduced. These factors must also be considered. The key is to find out what growth rate was projected in the past by the sales manager and to compare that to the actual growth rate. This will determine if his estimates were on target.

In our case, we have learned that over the past year, Mr. Williams had projected a 2% growth rate compared to an actual rate of 1% during the past three months. This, in itself, doesn't make the 2% estimate wrong. It does, however, signal the need for further analysis. Subsequent discussions with Mr. Williams revealed that the company has entered into a new contract with the government to ship 500 units per month beginning in August. Mr. Williams further indicated that the 2% growth rate was an average. Due to the seasonality of the air-conditioning business, sales growth is heaviest in the months of May through August. During this period a 3% growth rate over the previous December's sales is anticipated. In the other months, a 1% rate, exclusive of government sales, is expected.

WHAT IS TOTAL SALES VALUE?

How to Project Sales Value

Once we have projected the number of units to be sold, the determination of sales value is simply a matter of pricing out the sales. A good place to start is current prices. These can be obtained by reviewing invoices and price manuals. Make sure that forecast assumptions are sensitive to future changes, such as revised price lists, preferential pricing for certain customers, anticipated price increases, etc. Through discussions with marketing personnel, we have learned that beginning April 1, MBL is anticipating a 10% price increase over the current per unit price of $100. We have also learned that a special price of $95 per unit was negotiated for the new government contract.

Computation of Sales Value

Using the above assumptions, we are now ready to compute forecasted sales. Detailed computation schedules should be prepared for each product line and then summarized on a master forecasting schedule. Each computation schedule should be set up in enough detail to allow each component that is subject to a different forecast assumption to be evaluated separately. For example, the growth rate and pricing structure are different for both government and consumer contracts. Therefore, computation schedules should reflect these differences. The schedule shown in Table 2-1 is used to forecast consumer contract sales.

A word of caution on growth rates. We have assumed a compounded growth rate of 1% increasing to 3% during the summer months. This assumes a continued increase over base sales of 2,000 units. This assumption is fine if only the growth rate and not actual units sold declines in "nonsummer" months (i.e., sales decreases in New York during December are offset by sales in Florida). However, if sales actually decline during certain months, our assumptions would be incorrect and the calculations would have to be adjusted accordingly.

The sales value of government contracts can be calculated without the aid of a detailed schedule since no growth is forecasted. We have been

Table 2-1

MBL Mfg. Co.
Compounded Sales Value Calculations for Consumer Contracts for the Year Ended December 31, 19X1

Month	Growth Rate	Sales Quantity		Unit Prices	Sales Value
Current (base)	—	2,000		$100	$ —
January	1%	2,020	(2,000 × 101%)	100	202,000
February	1%	2,040	(2,020 × 101%)	100	204,000
March	1%	2,061	(2,040 × 101%)	100	206,100
April	1%	2,082	(2,061 × 101%)	110*	229,020
May	3%	2,144	(2,082 × 103%)	110*	235,840
June	3%	2,208	(2,144 × 103%)	110*	242,880
July	3%	2,274	(2,208 × 103%)	110*	250,140
August	3%	2,342	(2,274 × 103%)	110*	257,620
September	1%	2,365	(2,342 × 101%)	110*	260,150
October	1%	2,389	(2,365 × 101%)	110*	262,790
November	1%	2,413	(2,389 × 101%)	110*	265,430
December	1%	2,437	(2,413 × 101%)	110*	268,070
		26,775			$2,884,040

*Reflects 10% price increase.

Table 2-2

MBL Mfg. Co.
Noncompounded Sales Value Calculations for Consumer Contracts for the Year Ended December 31, 19X1

Month	Prior-Year Sales		Growth Rate		Sales Quantity	Unit Price	Sales Value
	Normal	Seasonal	Normal	Seasonal			
January	1,956		1%		1,976	100	$ 197,600
February	2,042		1%		2,062	100	206,200
March	2,005		1%		2,025	100	202,500
April	2,182	289	1%	3%	2,502	110	275,220
May	2,074	283	1%	3%	2,386	110	262,460
June	1,938	278	1%	3%	2,243	110	246,730
July	2,156	342	1%	3%	2,530	110	278,300
August	2,154		1%		2,176	110	239,360
September	2,183		1%		2,205	110	242,550
October	1,843		1%		1,861	110	204,710
November	1,985		1%		2,005	110	220,550
December	1,976		1%		1,996	110	219,560
					25,967		$2,795,740

told that government sales of 500 units per month will begin in August at a specially negotiated cash price of $95 per unit. Therefore:

Units sold per month	500
Number of months (Aug. through Dec.)	× 5
	2,500
Price per unit	$ 95
	$237,500

The above calculations presume a compounded growth factor. Another way of forecasting sales volume is to overlay a growth factor onto prior-year sales. In using this method, it is often advisable to separate seasonal sales from "normal" sales. We can then project sales volume as shown in Table 2-2.

Balance Sheet and Income Statement Effects

We have now successfully projected total sales for the year. At this point, nothing has happened to cash. However, since we have been asked to prepare an income statement and a balance sheet to accompany our cash flow projections, this is a good time to post the effect of sales on these statements. Turn to the forecasting worksheet (Exhibit 2-1). You will see that the above transactions are reflected as sales on the income statement. Even if cash is not received, the sale must be recorded for accounting purposes. Since no cash has been received, these transactions are reflected on the balance sheet as Accounts Receivable.

Once we have posted our transactions, we are ready to begin analyzing the cash position.

WHAT AMOUNT, IF ANY, REPRESENTS CASH SALES?

We have learned through conversations with Helen Brooks, the credit manager, that MBL sells all merchandise on 2/10, net/60 terms. This means a customer is entitled to a 2% discount if invoices are paid within 10 days. However, all payments are due within 60 days. Miss Brooks had further explained that in the current business environment, none of her customers paid cash. However, MBL was in the process of negotiating an all-cash contract with the government.

Since we have already independently verified the existence and quantity of government sales, we can now record cash collections on such sales. Again, if we turn to Exhibit 2-1, we can see how these collections affect cash (debit Cash and credit Accounts Receivable). This transaction achieves the same result as if we initially recorded a cash sale.

WHEN IS CASH CONTRACTUALLY DUE?

Forecasting Cash Receipts on Current-Year Sales

We have already been told that commercial customers, with the exception of those taking advantage of the discounts, pay after 60 days. In order to determine the amount of cash that will be received on accounts receivable, a schedule of expected cash receipts should be prepared. The easiest way to accomplish this is to prepare an expected cash receipts table based on the assumption that all customers will pay on the 60th day. Later we can adjust these figures for anticipated discounts. All balances should be broken down into as many categories as possible. This will simplify the calculations. For example, if we were told that most sales were 2/10, net/60 but there were certain sales that were sold on 2/10, net/30 terms, we would divide total sales into two categories, those due in 30 days and those due in 60 days. We would then prepare the schedule shown in Table 2-3 for each category of sale and post to the forecasting worksheet (Exhibit 2-1).

Table 2-3

MBL Mfg. Co.

Expected Cash Receipts on Sales During 19X1

	Amount and Month of Collection	
Sale Date	**19X1**	**19X2**
Jan.	$ 202,000—Mar.	
Feb.	204,000—Apr.	
Mar.	206,100—May	
Apr.	229,020—June	
May	235,840—July	
June	242,880—Aug.	
July	250,140—Sept.	
Aug.	257,620—Oct.	
Sept.	260,150—Nov.	
Oct.	262,790—Dec.	
Nov.		$ 265,430—Jan. 19X3
Dec.		268,070—Feb. 19X3
	$2,350,540	$533,500

Note that this schedule forecasts the payment of sales made in November and December in the subsequent period since cash is not contractually due for 60 days from the date of sale and since we have assumed that all customer payments are made on the 60th day.

However, let us assume that after reviewing the aged trial balance we note that although customers were required to pay within 60 days, the average age of an account receivable for individuals not taking discounts was 70 days. Let us further assume that sales do not take place evenly throughout the month and that 20% of sales take place in the first 10 days of the month, 30% in the second 10 days, and 50% in the last 10 days. Our expected cash receipts table could be modified as shown in Table 2-4.

Table 2-4
MBL Mfg. Co.
Expected Cash Receipts
on Sales During 19X1 (Modified)

Sale Date	Amount and Month of Collection		
	19X1		**19X2**
Jan.	$202,000—Mar.		
Feb.	204,000—Apr.		
Mar.	206,100—May		
Apr.	229,020—June		
May	235,840—July		
June	242,880—Aug.		
July	250,140—Sept.		
Aug.	257,620—Oct.		
Sept. (1–10)	52,030 (20% × $260,150)—Nov.		
(11–20)	78,045 (30% × 260,150)—Nov.		
(21–30)	130,075 (50% × 260,150)—Nov.		
Oct. (1–10)	52,558 (20% × 262,790)—Dec.		
(11–20)	78,837 (30% × 262,790)—Dec.		
(21–31)	(50% × 262,790)	$131,395—Dec.	
Nov.		265,430—Jan. 19X3	
Dec.		268,070—Feb. 19X3	
	$2,219,145	$664,895	

Note that it is not necessary to allocate sales for each month, since January sales collected within 70 days by definition will fall within 19X1 and December sales collected within 70 days will fall with 19X2. It is merely necessary to find the month or months which straddle both years.

The schedule could be further modified to assume that 40% of sales in a given period are collected after 70 days while 60% are collected after 50 days. To illustrate, let us prepare an expected cash receipts table for sales made in the month of October.

MBL Mfg. Co.
Expected Cash Receipts on Sales During October
19X1

Sale Date	Collections	
	19X1	19X2
October (1–10)	$ 21,023 (20% × $262,790 × 40%)	
(1–10)	31,535 (20% × 262,790 × 60%)	
(11–20)	31,535 (30% × 262,790 × 40%)	
(11–20)	47,302 (30% × 262,790 × 60%)	
(21–30)	(50% × 262,790 × 40%)	$52,558
(21–30)	78,837 (50% × 262,790 × 60%)	
	$210,232	$52,558

Since we have been asked to prepare only annual forecasted statements, an allocation between the current year (19X1) and the subsequent year (19X2) is adequate. If we had been asked to prepare monthly or quarterly statements, we could have included twelve monthly or four quarterly collection columns rather than one annual column. However, the same allocation principle would apply.

Forecasting Receipts on Prior-Year Sales

It is not sufficient to address only current sales because cash will also be received on existing outstanding accounts. Therefore, we must now determine if any cash will be received on prior-period sales. The easiest method to calculate these collections is to obtain an analysis of the opening balance of accounts receivable and schedule collections. Each component of beginning accounts receivable should be analyzed, and its collection should be forecasted and posted to the forecasting worksheet.

Let's look at the analysis of MBL's beginning accounts receivable balance.

MBL Mfg. Co.
Collection Schedule of Opening Accounts Receivable

Description	Collection Period	Amount
November sales	January 19X1	$195,000
December sales	February 19X1	198,000
XYZ Corp.	$5,000 per month plus interest	75,000
Sales prior to November	Past due	10,000
		$478,000

First, let's determine how November and December sales will affect our current year's cash. If these sales represent normal receivables (payment made on the 60th day), we can forecast them as collected in the current year. This will increase cash flow and decrease our receivable balance. Let's assume these sales have been collected. We can now post these collections of $195,000 and $198,000 to the forecasting worksheet (Exhibit 2-1).

Forecasting Principal and Interest Receipts on Past Due Accounts

Next, let's analyze the XYZ Corporation receivable. When we spoke to Miss Brooks, the credit manager, she mentioned that although MBL does not usually provide financing, one of the company's older customers, XYZ Corporation, was in financial trouble. Although MBL had stopped dealing with them, they were paying off their balance in monthly installments of $5,000 plus 11% interest on the outstanding balance. Now we must determine the collectibility of this receivable. First, we should determine whether XYZ is currently making the required monthly payments. If they are making the required payments, then it would be advisable to review their financial statements and/or make independent inquiries as to their ability to continue payment.

Once we are satisfied that the receivable will be collected, we must quantify the cash that will be received. Since XYZ, in addition to paying $60,000 of the receivable amount ($5,000 per month for 12 months), is also paying interest each month at an annual interest rate of 11%, we must calculate the amount of interest that MBL will receive during the current year. This can be done in a number of ways. First, we could prepare the actual interest calculations for each of the 12 months:

MBL Mfg. Co.
Interest Calculations on XYZ Corp. Receivable for 19X1

Month	Balance at Beginning of Month	Principal Payment	Balance at End of Month	Monthly Interest at .0092 (11% ÷ 12)
January	$75,000	$5,000	$70,000	$ 690
February	70,000	5,000	65,000	644
March	65,000	5,000	60,000	598
December	20,000	5,000	15,000	184
				$5,246*

Second, we could calculate interest based on the average balance outstanding:

Balance beginning of year	$75,000
Balance end of year	15,000
	90,000
To average	÷ 2
	45,000
Annual interest rate	11%
Total interest income	$ 4,950*

Third, we could calculate interest using the appropriate compound interest tables. The use of these tables will be explained in the Appendix.

Regardless of the method used, once we have calculated the annual interest due, we should then post both the principal and interest to the forecasting worksheet (Exhibit 2-1).

WHAT AMOUNT OF CASH IS COLLECTIBLE?

Factors Affecting Collectibility

Collection of past due accounts is definitely a function of management philosophy. First, we must ascertain whether projected sales growth is the result of lowering credit standards. This may not be bad if management is trying to move old or outdated stock or if gross profit on sales is high enough to offset increased bad debts. In either case, projected cash receipts should give effect to anticipated uncollectible sales as a result of these activities.

Second, we must also determine that the person who projected sales in the forecast period has evaluated changes in external economic conditions. For example, if borrowing rates are high, this will affect the timing of cash collections. To the extent that their borrowing costs become prohibitive, many purchasers tend to postpone their payments. This trend can be easily spotted by reviewing aging schedules of accounts receivable to determine if vendors are taking longer than normal to pay. External borrowing rates will also affect the amount of discounts taken by customers. The relationship of cash collections, discounts, and borrowing rates will be discussed in more detail later on in this chapter when we cover discounts.

Industry trends, as well as interest rates, must also be evaluated. Credit managers should be aware, at the very least, of the financial status of major customers. If customers tend to be in a particular industry, trends

---

*The difference between $5,246 and $4,950 is due to rounding. Since the difference is immaterial, either calculated amount can be used in the forecast.

in that industry should be carefully observed. For example, if you sell lumber for single-family homes or manufacture automobile parts, you should be aware of any decrease in new housing starts or the closing of automobile plants. These events might signal prolonged repayment periods for receivables, if not an actual reduction in sales.

Third, we must examine the effectiveness of collection efforts on past due accounts. Does management actively pursue delinquent accounts? A conscious decision may have been made not to pursue certain accounts if they are small and collection efforts may not be cost-justified. These accounts should be written off. However, whether or not these accounts are written off, their collection should not be projected.

We must also evaluate if collection efforts have been successful. The key here is to determine the percent of past due accounts that have been collected and when they were collected. We have been told that MBL's delinquent receivables are immaterial and consequently, no collection efforts are made. Because of the high cost of collection and the immateriality of the delinquent accounts, MBL has elected not to forecast any collection on past due receivables.

Effect of Sales Returns and Allowances on Collectibility

Sales returns and allowances also affect the collectibility of cash. Basically, sales returns and allowances fit into two broad categories, returns due to damaged or unacceptable merchandise and returns due to customer dissatisfaction. Merchandise falling under the first category of returns is usually reshipped. Therefore, it represents not a reduction in total sales but rather an increase in cost of goods sold (that is, new inventory shipped). The effect of these returns will be covered in detail under "Inventories" (Chapter 4).

The second type of return usually occurs with retail sales where the customers are individuals rather than corporations. Here, too, management philosophy must be reviewed. Are all sales final or is the customer guaranteed a "free trial period" with a full money-back refund if he or she is not totally satisfied? Once again, past experience and discussions with personnel in charge of customer returns should be used to forecast sales returns.

Since MBL has a proven product, it will replace goods only if they are damaged. As we mentioned above, this will affect cost of goods sold and, therefore, no adjustment would be required to our sales forecast. However, let's assume that MBL projected a 1% sales return due to dissatisfaction. Using our previous forecasting worksheet format, this adjustment would be simple. Total sales would be reduced by 1% ($2,884,040 × 1% = $28,840 [Exhibit 2-1]). Total cash receipts would also be reduced by 1% ($2,350,540 × 1% = $23,505 [Exhibit 2-1]) since we had previously forecasted 100% collection within 60 days.

WHAT AMOUNT OF CASH IS DUE?

How to Project Discounts

Obviously, by allowing customers a discount on merchandise there is a good possibility that the full sales price will not be ultimately collected. For MBL, this amount could reduce cash by $47,010 ($2,350,540 × 2%) and total sales by $56,800 ($2,840,040 × 2%). Since total available cash and net income for a company of this size may total only $200,000 to $300,000, these discounts could be quite significant to the company. For example, if MBL had gross sales of $3,000,000 and net income of $200,000, a 2% discount on sales would reduce net income by $60,000, or 30% ($60,000 ÷ $200,000).

Our first step in quantifying potential discounts is to identify the sales that are subject to a discount. We have previously learned from the credit manager that sales to the government are at a specially negotiated cash price and, therefore, are not subject to discounts. Consequently, only consumer sales, which we have forecasted at $2,840,040, are subject to discounts.

Factors Affecting Discounts

In order to calculate the portion of these sales that will be discounted, let's consider some of the factors that affect discounts:

1. *Cost of the customer's borrowed funds versus the amount of the discount.* The amount of discount taken is primarily a function of the purchaser's borrowing rate. When the seller ships merchandise to a customer and the customer is not required to pay cash, the seller is financing the customer's inventory. A customer who does not owe the seller the cash for 60 days has, in essence, a 60-day interest-free loan. When the seller gives a customer the option of paying a reduced price (2/10, net/60), the seller is telling the customer that the cash sales price is 98% and the finance charge is 2%.

Another way of looking at this is that the customer is paying 2% for the right to retain his or her cash for 50 days (the customer is paying 2% to borrow the funds for 50 days). This works out to an effective rate of .04% per day (2% ÷ 50 days), or 14.4% per year (.04% × 360 days). If the customer has to borrow at a rate higher than 14.4%, he or she is better off borrowing from the seller, that is, waiting the full 60 days to pay. The converse is also true. If it costs the seller more than 14.4% to borrow money, the seller is losing money by financing the customer's inventory. This concept of the *cost of idle funds* will be explained in more detail in Chapter 3. Also, Chapter 3 will discuss some of the techniques of determining prime rates.

2. *Customer mentality.* Some unsophisticated customers always take discounts, regardless of the economics, because they think they are getting a bargain. In fact, making this impression is one of the key reasons a discount is given. On the other hand, there are also customers that never take advantage of discounts because their paying cycle is longer than the allowable discount period or because they lack effective cash management.

3. *Major customers.* Some customers, usually large or significant ones, believe they are entitled to a discount, regardless of when they pay their bills. Management philosophy is important here. From a cash management standpoint, the company must decide whether these customers will be allowed to keep the discount. Loss of the discount must be weighed against the potential loss of the customer.

Computation of Discounts

In our conversation with Miss Brooks, we were told that discounts taken at MBL were solely a function of the customer's borrowing cost versus the discount rate. Since a 2% discount can be earned by paying 50 days early, this translates into an effective annual rate of 14.4%.

Let's assume that the prime rate through August will be well in excess of 14.4%. Then, in September, the prime rate will drop to below 14%. This means customers are not likely to be taking discounts until September of the upcoming year.

Now that we have identified the sales that are likely to be discounted, we must calculate the effect of these discounts on our cash forecast. A discount will have a twofold effect on our forecast. First, it will reduce collections by the 2% discount rate. Second, it will accelerate collections by 50 days. To calculate these efforts let's use the worksheet format presented in Table 2-5.

Let's assume that $180,000 of MBL's December sales are projected to

Table 2-5

MBL Mfg. Co.

Calculation of Effect of 2% Discount on Cash for the Year 19X1

Sales Month	Gross Sales Amount	Sales Net of 1% Returns	2% Discount	Old Collection Period	Old Gross Collection Amount	Collections Net of 1% Returns	New Collection Period	New Collection Amount at 98%
Sept.	$260,150	$257,548	$ 5,150	19X1	$260,150	$257,548	19X1	$252,397
Oct.	262,790	260,162	5,203	19X1	262,790	260,162	19X1	254,959
Nov.	265,430	262,776	5,256	19X2	—	—	19X1	257,520
Dec.	268,070	265,389	5,308	19X2	—	—	19X1	176,400*
			$20,917			$517,710		$941,276

*Sales made through December 20, if collected within 10 days, would impact 19X1 cash receipts. Therefore, we must determine the amount of sales generated from December 1 to December 20.

occur during the first 20 days of the month. Then $176,400 ($180,000 × 98%) would be collected in 19X1.

At this point, we are now ready to adjust our forecasting worksheet (Exhibit 2-1) as follows:

1. Overall Sales and Accounts Receivable must be reduced by $20,917.

2. September through December's collections must be adjusted to reflect the accelerated cash receipts due to the discount taken. This can best be done in two steps. First, remove September through December cash receipts previously recorded on the forecasting worksheet ($517,710 net of the 1% return). Second, record the revised forecasted receipts ($941,276) on the forecasting worksheet.

This technique of recording our projections gross and subsequently making changes or corrections gross (removing previous month's receipts gross and substituting the revised or adjusted gross receipts) is significant to the forecasting process. As we will discuss in Chapter 9, forecasts are most useful when they can respond to a series of "what if" questions and to changes in assumptions. When the gross technique is used throughout the forecasting process, we have not only a trail of the changes made but workpapers that easily facilitate further adjustments and refinements of the projections. This promotes flexibility in the forecasting process.

Use of Ratios and Averages

The first portion of this chapter discussed a step-by-step approach to annually projecting the sales area of a forecast. This approach can effectively be used by a company of any size that has undiversified product lines or that has a computer capable of preparing and summarizing these individual calculation schedules for a few hundred products. However, what do we do for a company with diverse product lines and no computer capability? The remainder of this chapter will explain some statistical formulas and shortcuts that can be used to achieve results relatively similar to the first approach we used.

The methods that can be used to forecast a complex sales area depend almost entirely on the degree of preciseness required in the forecast. Regardless of mathematical accuracy, forecasts are entirely dependent on the predictability and accuracy of their underlying assumptions. How accurate would our forecast be if a 2% growth rate was calculated to 10 decimal places and the actual growth rate was 5%? Never attempt to achieve a level of mathematical accuracy that cannot be supported by the same degree of predictability or accuracy of the underlying assumptions.

Depending on the nature of the forecast and the degree of accuracy desired, averages and ratios can be effectively used in calculating projections. The following items may be used individually or in combination with one another:

COMPOUND FINANCIAL TABLES

In forecasting MBL's sales for the year, we calculated a 1% and a 3% growth rate compounded monthly. In order to calculate annual sales, we did 12 separate calculations, beginning with a starting sales figure of 2,000 units per month (2,000 × 101% = 2,020; 2,020 × 101% = 2,040; etc.). Another method that can be used to obtain the same result is the compound financial tables technique. Although the Appendix will explain in detail the concepts and use of these tables, a brief discussion of their use is appropriate here. By using the "amount of 1" in the 1% and 3% table, we can get the same answer obtained by our first approach but with far fewer calculations. For example:

Starting sales volume	2,000	
4-mo. growth factor @ 1%	4.10100	8,202
Sales volume end of month four	2,081	
4-mo. growth factor @ 3%	4.30913	8,967
Sales volume end of month eight	2,341	
4-mo. growth factor @ 1%	4.10100	9,600
Total sales		26,769

With the exception of a 6-unit rounding difference (26,769 vs. 26,775), we have obtained the same result with three rather than twelve calculations.

AVERAGES

The previous three calculations can be further reduced to one calculation by the use of an average growth rate. For example:

Base sales volume (Dec.)	2,000
12-mo. Aug. growth factor @ $1^{21}\!/_{32}$*	13.155784
Total Sales	26,312

*$1^{21}\!/_{32}$% represents the compound financial table closest to $1\frac{5}{8}$%, the average growth rate. This average growth rate is calculated as follows:

1% growth for 4 months =	4
3% growth for 4 months =	12
1% growth for 4 months =	4
	20
To average	÷ 12
	1.666 = $1\frac{5}{8}$

Although the differences increase from 6 to 463 (26,775 − 26,312), this difference is less than 2% and still immaterial, compared to the total projected units.

Another averaging technique that can be used is to apply an overall growth rate to prior year's sales. When we talked to Mr. Williams, the sales manager, he informed us that his overall growth rate of 2% was an annual average which took into account heavy growth during the summer months. Since this projected average rate allows for seasonal fluctuations, we can apply the rate to the total number of units sold in the previous year, and get a realistic projection.

We can also use the averaging technique to calculate new unit prices. Since MBL's unit price of $100 is expected to increase to $110 per unit on April 1, this would equate to an average unit price of $107.50, calculated as follows:

$100 per mo. for 3 months =	$ 300.00
$110 per mo. for 9 months =	990.00
	1,290.00
To average	÷ 12
Average unit price	$ 107.50

For MBL, this would translate into a total sales value of $2,878,312 (26,775 units × $107.50). The difference between this sales value and our detailed monthly price-out of $2,884,040 is only $5,728, quite immaterial when compared to total sales of roughly $3 million.

RATIOS

Our tables of expected cash receipts (Tables 2-3 and 2-4) calculate, on a month-by-month basis, sales which are expected to be collected in the current year and those which are expected to be collected in the following year. Collections anticipated in the following year will be accounts receivable at the end of the current year. Therefore, if we subtract expected accounts receivable from total projected sales, we can forecast sales collections. One way of projecting accounts receivable is by the use of the following days sales outstanding (DSO) ratio:

$$\frac{\text{Average current receivable balance 3 month-ends} \times 90}{\text{Credit sales for the same 3 month-ends}}$$

For example, if the last three months' sales totaled $727,000 and the average accounts receivable balance for the same three-month period was $560,000, DSO would be calculated as follows:

$$\frac{560,000 \times 90}{727,000} = 69.33 \text{ days}$$

Once the number of days sales outstanding is calculated, we can use this to forecast future sales. For example, if MBL has forecasted $2,884,040 of credit sales for next year, then total collections for the year could be calculated as follows:

$$\frac{360 - 69.33}{360} \times \$2,884,040 = \$2,328,622$$

The above method of projecting sales permits us to give effect for the actual number of days it has historically taken to collect a receivable rather than merely the contractual terms. It should be noted that before this method is used, a review should be made to determine that the sample period selected is representative of an entire year. An alternative is to use a full one year as the sample period. Also, we should determine that the environment during the forecast period is expected to be the same as the sample period, i.e., sales terms and creditworthiness of purchasers are similar.

Exhibit 2-1
MBL Mfg. Co.
Forecasting Worksheet for the Year Ended 12/31/19X1

	Cash Flow			Income Statement		Balance Sheet		
	Sales	Collections On Accounts Receivable	Interest Receipts	Sales	Interest Income	Cash	Accounts Receivable	Retained Earnings
Consumer sales				$2,884,040			$ 2,884,040	$2,884,040
Government sales	$237,500			237,500			237,500	237,500
Cash received—govt. sales						$ 237,500	(237,500)	
Collections on accounts receivable		$2,350,540				2,350,540	(2,350,540)	
Prior-year sales:								
November		195,000				195,000	(195,000)	
December		198,000				198,000	(198,000)	
Collections from XYZ Corp:								
Principal		60,000				60,000	(60,000)	
Interest			$4,950		$4,950	4,950		4,950
1% sales return				(28,840)			(28,840)	(28,840)
Effect on cash of 1% sales return		(23,505)				(23,505)	23,505	
2% sales discount				(20,917)			(20,917)	(20,917)
Effect on cash of 2% sales discount		(517,710)				(517,710)	517,710	
		941,276				941,276	(941,276)	
	$237,500	$3,203,601	$4,950	$3,071,783	$4,950	$3,446,051	$ (369,318)	$3,076,733

Money Market Investments

For purposes of our discussion, we will define money market investments as funds invested in interest-bearing obligations for the purpose of earning current income, not for capital appreciation.

Companies usually maintain funds in this type of investment for two reasons:

1. It is their industry (i.e., banks, money market funds, pension plans, investment banking firms, brokerage firms, etc.). These firms invest in money market instruments because their return (interest income) is greater than their cost of funds and therefore they make a profit. For example, a savings and loan association borrows funds in the form of savings deposits at a cost of, say, 5½%, invests them in mortgages at, say, 13%, and makes a profit of roughly 7½% less operating expenses.

2. It is an income-producing way to invest funds until they can be employed for a "higher and better use." For example, a builder who obtains a down payment on the construction of a building may invest in money market instruments until the cash is needed to purchase materials or pay overhead. A manufacturing company may invest in money market instruments until the funds are required to buy raw materials or meet debt obligations.

Types of Money Market Instruments

Money market instruments are usually classified according to their length of maturity or their payment schedule.

LENGTH OF MATURITY

Money market investments can be classified into three broad categories: short-term, long-term, and intermediate-term.

Short-Term Investments

Short-term investments usually refer to obligations maturing in less than 90 days. Typically, this category of investments includes the following:

- Savings accounts
- Certificates of deposit (interest-bearing bank certificates)
- Treasury bills
- Commercial paper (short-term corporate notes)
- Repurchase agreements (Repos)

Long-Term Investments

Long-term investments usually refer to obligations maturing in more than one year. Some of the more common investments falling into this category include the following:

- Treasury bonds and notes
- Municipal bonds
- Corporate bonds
- Mortgages

Intermediate-Term Investments

Intermediate-term investments usually refer to obligations maturing between three months and one year. Investments in this category consist of a mix of what we've classified as both short-term and long-term investments. As an example, an intermediate investment may include a corporate or municipal bond maturing in nine months. Treasury bills can also be purchased with nine-month maturities.

Although few people would say that a 20-year mortgage is short-term, intermediate investments may be considered either short-term or long-term, depending on the type of investor. For example, a manufacturing company investing funds while awaiting an inventory shipment might consider six months a long-term investment. On the other hand, a bank granting 30-year mortgages might easily consider the same type of six-month investment as short-term.

Short-Term versus Long-Term Investments

The decision to go short-term versus long-term is usually a function of the following criteria.

Yield. How much can be earned on the cash? Yield is a determinant of:

1. Time—usually the longer an obligation is outstanding, the lower the yield.
2. Risk—usually the riskier an obligation, the higher the yield.

The actual rate earned on any investment is a combination of the above. For example, a long-term highly speculative corporate bond may have a much higher rate than a short-term Treasury bill.

Economic Projections. If yields are expected to decline in the near future, investments in longer-term obligations will ensure a maximum return on investment during the period. However, if yields are expected to rise in the near future, investments in shorter-term obligations will ensure the availability of funds to utilize in the future for higher yields.

Cost of Idle Funds. With the exception of those companies whose business it is to invest in market instruments, it is presumed that funds can better be used in the operation of one's own business. To the extent that General Motors can make more money lending funds than it can making cars, it is no longer in the automotive business but in the banking business. However, if General Motors has money in a non-interest-bearing account awaiting delivery of a steel shipment, it is losing money.

Since most short-term obligations bear significant penalties for early redemption, it is vital to time required payments, like those for GM's steel shipments, to the maturity of the obligation in order to maximize the yield on the short-term investment. As we discussed in Chapter 1, it therefore becomes imperative that we properly forecast the peaks and valleys of cash flow in order to maximize yields on such investments.

Alternate Uses of Funds. As already mentioned, a builder or manufacturer is not in the business of lending money. Therefore, before any funds are invested in money market instruments, the following alternatives should be considered:

1. Purchase of additional inventory at quantity discounts
2. Payment of outstanding invoices at discounts
3. Payment of existing bank or other outstanding debt, thus reducing interest expense

4. Increase in production
5. Expansion of property plant and equipment
6. Expansion of research and development

PAYMENT SCHEDULE

Money market investments can be further categorized and forecasted according to their payment schedule.

1. Obligations with principal and interest due at maturity—for example, certificates of deposit and Treasury bills. Interest on such obligations may or may not be compounded. (Interest is earned on unpaid interest.)
2. Obligations on which principal is due at maturity and interest is paid periodically—for example, municipal and corporate bonds.
3. Self-amortizing obligations paying periodic principal and interest—for example, a mortgage.

Most of the above obligations can be purchased at face on an initial offering (i.e., when they are first sold) or at a discount or premium in the secondary market (i.e., when they are resold).

The concept of discounting is both an economic and an accounting concept and not a cash flow concept. For example, a $1,000 corporate bond with a coupon rate of 6% may be purchased for $900 to yield 8%. The only effect on cash is the purchase price. Both bonds, if held to maturity, will repay $1,000 in principal. In addition, annual cash of $60 ($1,000 × 6%) will be received, regardless of the purchase price. Economically, however, it is better to earn $60 a year on a $900 investment rather than $60 a year on a $1,000 investment.

Accountants, on the other hand, would prefer to reflect $72 in interest income ($60 in cash and $12 in amortization of discount). For illustrative purposes, since this text deals with cash flow and not generally accepted accounting principles, all discounts will be amortized using the straight-line method over the life of the obligation, not the interest method required by generally accepted accounting principles.

Forecasting Money Market Investments

Your review of MBL's investment ledger reveals the money market investments shown in Table 3-1. Your initial discussion with Tom Blake, vice-president in charge of money management, indicated that the company's intent is to hold all investments until maturity and to maintain at least $10,000 in CDs at all times, regardless of how excess funds may be employed.

In addition, you have learned that the company took back a $1,500,000 25-year self-amortizing mortgage on the sale of an obsolete warehouse in 1978. The mortgage pays interest at the rate of 12% per year. Interest and principal payments are due the first of each month.

Table 3-1
MBL Mfg. Co.
Money Market Investments

Bank	Principal Amount	Cost	Coupon	Purchase Date	Interest Payment Dates	Maturity
Bank of N.Y. CD	$ 10,000	$ 10,000	10%	11/10/19X0	6 mo. pd. at maturity	5/10/19X1
Bank of N.Y. CD	$ 15,000	$ 15,000	11¼%	12/15/19X0	6 mo. pd. at maturity	6/15/19X1
First Boston	$ 10,000	$ 10,000	10½%	12/15/19X0	12 mo. pd. at maturity	12/15/19X1
Chemical Bank (savings a/c)	$ 10,560	$ 10,000	5¼%	12/1/19X0	Compounded monthly	—
T-bill	$ 20,000	$ 19,575	9.04%	12/15/19X0	Maturity	3/15/19X1
T-bill	$ 15,000	$ 14,250	9.89%	12/1/19X0	Maturity	6/1/19X1
XYZ Corp.	$100,000	$100,000	12%	6/13/1978	Jan. 1 and July 1	1/1/2000
ABC Corp.	$500,000	$485,000	7¼%	5/20/1974	May 15 and Nov. 15	5/15/1994
New Jersey Power	$300,000	$300,000	10%	6/15/19X0	June 15 and Dec. 15	6/15/19X1

Since cash flow is a function of the receipt of principal and/or interest, money market investments can affect cash flow in three ways:

1. Principal and interest are received during the cash forecast period.
2. Interest only is received during the cash forecast period and principal is received subsequently.
3. Neither principal nor interest is received during the cash forecast period.

Cash flow projections should be made for each of the above categories and posted to the forecasting worksheet (Exhibit 3-1). Since we have been asked to prepare an income statement and a balance sheet, in addition to a cash forecast, we should be cognizant of income that is earned but not paid (accrued) during the forecast period.

CERTIFICATES OF DEPOSIT

The first step in our forecasting process is to calculate expected cash receipts on CDs, as shown in Table 3-2. Since current banking regulations prohibit the compounding of interest, the calculations are quite simple. Interest and principal are received in cash at the maturity of the CD. Interest, however, is accrued for accounting purposes based on the period of time the CD is outstanding during the forecast period.

Since company policy requires at least $10,000 to be maintained in CDs, let's assume that of the $15,000 CD maturing on June 15, $10,000 will be rolled over (reinvested) for six months at a 13% rate and that the same $10,000 CD will be rolled over again on December 15 at 14%. Your calculations would then be expanded as shown in Table 3-3.

Table 3-2
MBL Mfg. Co.
Expected Cash Receipts from Certificates of Deposit

Bank	Term	Maturity	Rate	Interest Accrued	Interest Paid in 19X1	Principal Paid in 19X1
Bank of New York	6 mo.	5/10/19X1	10%	$ 361	$ 500 (10,000 ×10% × 6/12) (10,000 ×10% × 130/360)	$10,000
Bank of New York	6 mo.	6/15/19X1	11½%	791	863 (15,000 ×11½% × 6/12) (15,000 × 11½% × 165/360)	15,000
First Boston	12 mo.	12/15/19X1	10½%	1,006	1,050 (10,000 × 10½ × 12/12) (10,000 ×10½ × 345/360)	10,000

Table 3-3
MBL Mfg. Co.
Expected Cash Receipts from Certificates of Deposit Including Rollovers

Bank	Term	Maturity	Rate	Interest Accrued	Interest Paid in 19X1	Principal Paid in 19X1
Bank of N.Y.	6 mo.	5/10/19X1	10%	$ 361	$ 500 (10,000 ×10% × 6/12) (10,000 ×10% × 130/360	$10,000
Bank of N.Y.	6 mo.	6/15/19X1	11½%	791	863 (15,000 ×11½% × 6/12) (15,000 × 11½% × 165/360)	15,000
First Boston	12 mo.	12/15/19X1	10½%	1,006	1,050 (10,000 × 10½ × 12/12) (10,000 ×10½% × 345/360)	10,000
Bank of N.Y.	6 mo.	6/15/19X1	11½%			(10,000)
Bank of N.Y.	6 mo.	12/15/19X1	13%	650	650 (10,000 ×13% × 6/12)	10,000
Bank of N.Y.	6 mo.	12/15/19X1	13%			(10,000)
Bank of N.Y.	6 mo.	12/15/19X1	14%	58	— (10,000 ×14% × 15/360)	—
				$2,866	$3,063	$25,000

When posting to the forecasting worksheet, it is often easiest to post accrued interest to a receivable account and correspondingly to recognize cash receipts as a reduction of the accrual, a procedure much like posting to a general ledger. This assures that there is no duplication of either income or cash flow.

SAVINGS ACCOUNTS

Since savings accounts do not have fixed maturities, no cash is contractually due throughout the forecast period. Since principal and interest may be drawn out at management's discretion we can program cash receipts and disbursements at will. For illustrative purposes, let us program a $5,000 deposit into the savings account on June 15, 19X1 and a $7,000 withdrawal from the account on December 15, 19X1. Since all interest earned is added to the savings account balance as accrued income, no distinction need be made as to cash principal or interest. Table 3-4 shows the calculations that can be made to determine cash receipts and interest income. We can now summarize this activity on the forecasting worksheet.

Table 3-4

MBL Mfg. Co.

Calculations of Savings Account Activity for 19X1

Period	Cash Deposited (Withdrawn)	Interest Earned	Balance
Beg. balance			$10,560
1/1–1/3	—	$ 49 (10,566 × 5.5% × 31/365)	10,609
2/1–2/28	—	45 (10,609 × 5.5% × 28/365)	10,654
3/1–3/31	—	50 (10,654 × 5.5% × 31/365)	10,704
4/1–4/30	—	48 (10,704 × 5.5% × 30/365)	10,752
5/1–5/31	—	50 (10,752 × 5.5% × 31/365)	10,802
6/1–6/15	—	24 (10,802 × 5.5% × 15/365)	10,826
6/15	5,000		15,826
6/16–6/30	—	36 (15,826 × 5.5% × 15/365)	15,862
7/1–7/31	—	74 (15,862 × 5.5% × 31/365)	15,936
8/1–8/31	—	74 (15,936 × 5.5% × 31/365)	16,010
9/1–9/30	—	72 (16,010 × 5.5% × 30/365)	16,082
10/1–10/31	—	75 (16,082 × 5.5% × 31/365)	16,157
11/1–11/30	—	73 (16,157 × 5.5% × 30/365)	16,230
12/1–12/15	—	37 (16,230 × 5.5% × 15/365)	16,267
12/15	(7,000)		9,267
12/16–12/31	—	22 (9,267 × 5.5% × 16/365)	9,289
	$(2,000)	$729	

The calculations shown in Table 3-4 can be greatly reduced by use of compound financial tables. When using these tables, there is no need to prorate the tables for deposits and withdrawals made during the month, rather than at the beginning or end of the month, since the differences will not be material. The calculations could therefore be made as follows:

Balance 1/1/19X1	$10,560	
Amount of $1 for 6 mo. (1.0278 − 1.0)	.0278	
		293
Balance 6/30/19X1 ($10,560 + 293 + 5,000)	15,853	
Amount of $1 for 5 mo. (1.0231 − 1.0)	.0231	
		366
Balance 12/1/19X1 ($15,853 + 366 − 7,000)	9,219	
Amount of $1 for 1 mo. (1.0046 − 1.0)	.0046	
		42
		$701
		vs.
		$729

The difference of $28 ($729 − $701) is the result of using whole months rather than prorating the June 15 and December 15 transactions and would be immaterial to the cash flow projection.

TREASURY BILLS

The next investment item to forecast is Treasury bills. Treasury bills do not pay interest per se but they are always sold at a discount and pay off at their face amount at maturity. Therefore, in order to project cash flow, we merely need to pick up the face amount of Treasury bills maturing within the forecast period. For purposes of the income statement, however, income is derived by amortizing the unearned discount as shown in Table 3-5. These totals can now be posted to the forecasting worksheet (Exhibit 3-1).

Table 3-5

MBL Mfg. Co.

Calculation of Amortization of Unearned Discount on Treasury Bills

Face	Cost	Discount	Term	Purchase Date	Income	Cash Received
$20,000	$19,575	$425	90 days	12/15/19X0	$354($425 × 75/90)	$20,000
15,000	14,250	750	180 days	12/15/19X0	625($750 × 150/180)	15,000
					$979	$35,000

CORPORATE AND MUNICIPAL BONDS

As Table 3-6 demonstrates, cash flow on corporate and municipal obligations is also a simple item to forecast. Here, interest is not compounded but is paid on specific dates, usually at six-month intervals, and principal is paid at maturity unless the obligation is sold.

Table 3-6

MBL Mfg. Co.

Expected Cash Receipts from Municipal and Corporate Bonds

Issuer	Principal Amount	Coupon	Payment Dates in 19X1		Cash Received	
					Interest	Principal
XYZ Corp.	$100,000	12%	2	(100,000 × 12%)	$12,000	$ —
ABC Corp.	500,000	7¼%	2	(500,000 × 7¼%)	36,250	—
N.J. Power	300,000	10%	1*	(300,000 × 10% × ½)	15,000	300,000
					$63,250	$300,000

*Remember that the N.J. Power bond matures on 6/15/19X1; therefore there is only one interest payment date in 19X1.

Again, since we are preparing an income statement in addition to a cash flow forecast, it is necessary to amortize the discount on corporate bonds into income. As we mentioned earlier, the $15,000 discount on ABC Corp. bonds is done on the straight line method, as follows:

$$\$500,000 - \$485,000 = \$15,000 \div 20 \text{ yrs} = \$750 \text{ per year}$$

A word of caution: The mere maturity of a bond does not ensure its redemption, nor does an interest payment date ensure the receipt of cash. Before either an interest or principal payment is forecasted, a review of the financial status of the issuer is in order. The following areas should be reviewed and considered before projecting the receipt of cash:

• Is the issuer in default as to interest?
• Is the issuer in default as to principal on any other issues?
• Does the issuer have the financial resources to pay the obligation on time?
• Is the issuer in default on any obligations that are senior to yours?
• Does the issuer's financial statements contain an auditor's opinion that is qualified as to refinancing these or any other debt obligations?
• Has the issuer attempted to unsuccessfully refinance these or any other debt obligations?
• Does a default on these obligations trigger a default on other debt obligations that are senior to yours?
• Has the issuer filed for bankruptcy?

Once we have satisfied ourselves as to the collectibility of interest and principal we can again post to the forecasting worksheet (Exhibit 3-1).

SELF-AMORTIZING OBLIGATIONS

Annual cash flow on self-amortizing obligations can easily be forecasted by simply multiplying the standard monthly payment by 12. For example, the standard monthly payment on a $1,500,000, 25-year, self-amortizing mortgage at 12% interest is $15,798. Therefore, total cash receipts can be calculated as follows:

Standard monthly payment	$ 15,798
No. of months in forecast period	× 12
	$189,576

There are several ways to determine the standard monthly payment:

1. Examine the note and/or mortgage obligation. It usually states all terms, including the standard payment.
2. Examine cash receipts to determine the amounts previously paid.
3. Calculate the standard monthly payment using compound financial tables as follows:

Original face amount of the obligation	$1,500,000
"Partial payment" factor using the 12% table	× .010532
Standard payment	$ 15,798

4. Look up the monthly payment necessary to amortize $1,500,000 over 25 years at 12% in a "Comprehensive Mortgage Payment" table as shown in Table 3-7.

If the table does not cover the amount of your loan, the payment can be interpolated. For example, a $100,000, 25-year loan at 12% would have a standard monthly payment of $1,053.23. Consequently, since a $1,500,000 loan is 15 times that of a $100,000 loan, its standard payment would be $1,053.23 × 15 = $15,798.45. Since we are preparing a balance sheet and an income statement in addition to a cash forecast, it is necessary to allocate principal and interest in the standard monthly payment. The easiest way to do this is to obtain an amortization table from any of the financial publishing companies. For a nominal fee, these publishers will prepare a table that illustrates the monthly allocation between principal and interest for the specific mortgage. This table also shows the outstanding principal balance being reduced with each payment. All amortization tables used should be a permanent part of the cash flow workpapers since they can

Table 3-7
Schedule of Monthly Payments Necessary to Amortize a Loan at 12%

			Term (Number of Years)				
Amount	19	20	21	22	23	24	25
$ 25	.28	.28	.28	.27	.27	.27	.27
50	.56	.56	.55	.54	.54	.54	.53
75	.84	.83	.82	.81	.81	.80	.79
100	1.12	1.11	1.09	1.08	1.07	1.07	1.06
200	2.24	2.21	2.18	2.16	2.14	2.13	2.11
300	3.35	3.31	3.27	3.24	3.21	3.19	3.16
400	4.47	4.41	4.36	4.32	4.28	4.25	4.22
500	5.58	5.51	5.45	5.39	5.35	5.31	5.27
600	6.70	6.61	6.54	6.47	6.42	6.37	6.37
700	7.81	7.71	7.63	7.55	7.48	7.43	7.38
800	8.93	8.81	8.71	8.63	8.55	8.49	8.43
900	10.04	9.91	9.80	9.71	9.62	9.55	9.48
1000	11.16	11.02	10.89	10.78	10.69	10.61	10.54
2000	22.31	22.03	21.78	21.56	21.38	21.21	21.07
3000	33.47	33.04	32.67	32.34	32.06	31.82	31.60
4000	44.62	44.05	43.55	43.12	42.75	42.42	42.13
5000	55.77	55.06	54.44	53.90	53.43	53.02	52.67
6000	66.93	66.07	65.33	64.68	64.12	63.63	63.20
7000	78.08	77.08	76.21	75.46	74.80	74.23	73.73
8000	89.24	88.09	87.10	86.24	85.49	84.84	84.26
9000	100.39	99.10	97.99	92.02	96.18	95.44	94.80
10000	111.54	110.11	108.87	107.80	106.86	106.04	105.33
11000	122.70	121.12	119.76	118.58	117.55	116.65	115.86
12000	133.85	132.14	130.65	129.36	129.23	127.25	126.39
13000	145.01	143.15	141.54	140.14	138.92	137.85	136.92
14000	156.16	154.16	152.42	150.92	149.60	148.46	147.46
15000	167.31	165.17	163.31	161.70	160.29	159.06	157.99
16000	178.47	176.18	174.20	172.48	170.98	169.67	168.52
17000	189.62	187.19	185.08	183.25	181.66	180.27	179.05
18000	200.77	198.20	195.97	194.03	192.35	190.87	189.59
19000	211.93	209.21	206.86	204.81	203.03	201.48	200.12
20000	223.08	220.22	217.74	215.59	213.72	212.08	210.64
21000	234.24	231.23	228.63	226.37	224.40	222.69	221.18
22000	245.39	242.24	239.52	237.15	235.09	233.29	231.71
23000	256.54	253.25	250.41	247.93	245.77	243.89	242.25
24000	267.70	264.27	261.29	258.71	256.46	254.50	252.78
25000	278.85	275.28	272.18	269.49	267.15	265.10	263.31
26000	290.01	286.29	283.07	280.27	277.83	275.70	273.84
27000	301.16	297.30	293.95	291.05	288.52	286.31	284.38
28000	312.31	308.31	304.84	301.83	299.20	296.91	294.91
29000	323.47	319.32	315.73	312.61	309.89	307.52	305.44
30000	334.62	330.33	326.61	323.39	320.57	318.12	315.97

Table 3-7 (cont.)

	Term (Number of Years)						
Amount	19	20	21	22	23	24	25
31000	345.77	341.34	337.50	334.17	331.26	328.72	326.50
32000	356.93	352.35	348.39	344.95	341.95	339.33	337.04
33000	368.08	363.36	359.28	355.72	352.63	349.93	347.57
34000	379.24	374.37	370.16	366.50	363.32	360.53	358.10
35000	390.39	385.39	381.05	377.28	374.00	371.14	368.63
40000	446.16	440.44	435.48	431.18	427.43	424.16	421.29
45000	501.93	495.49	489.92	485.08	480.86	477.18	473.96
50000	557.70	550.55	544.35	538.97	534.29	530.20	526.62
55000	613.47	605.60	598.79	592.87	587.72	583.22	579.28
60000	669.24	660.66	653.22	646.77	641.14	636.23	631.94
65000	725.01	715.71	707.66	700.66	694.57	689.25	684.60
70000	780.77	770.77	762.09	754.56	748.00	742.27	737.26
75000	836.54	825.82	816.53	808.46	801.43	795.29	789.92
80000	892.31	880.87	870.96	862.36	854.86	848.31	842.58
100000	1115.39	1101.09	1088.70	1077.94	1068.57	1060.39	1053.23

Table 3-8

MBL Mfg. Co.

Amortization Table for 19X1 of $1,500,000, 12%, 25-Year Loan

Month	Standard Payment	Interest	Principal	Balance after Application of Payment
End of prior year	(per general ledger)			$1,450,500
January	$ 15,798 (1,450,500 × 12% × 1/12)	$ 14,505	$ 1,293	1,449,207
February	15,798 (1,449,207 × 12% × 1/12)	14,492	1,306	1,447,901
March	15,798 (1,447,901 × 12% × 1/12)	14,479	1,319	1,446,582
April	15,798 (1,446,582 × 12% × 1/12)	14,466	1,332	1,445,250
May	15,798 (1,445,250 × 12% × 1/12)	14,453	1,345	1,443,905
June	15,798 (1,443,905 × 12% × 1/12)	14,439	1,359	1,442,546
July	15,798 (1,442,546 × 12% × 1/12)	14,425	1,373	1,441,173
August	15,798 (1,441,173 × 12% × 1/12)	14,412	1,386	1,439,787
September	15,798 (1,439,787 × 12% × 1/12)	14,398	1,400	1,438,387
October	15,798 (1,438,387 × 12% × 1/12)	14,384	1,414	1,436,973
November	15,798 (1,436,973 × 12% × 1/12)	14,370	1,428	1,435,545
December	15,798 (1,435,545 × 12% × 1/12)	14,355	1,443	1,434,102
	$189,576	$173,178	$16,398	

be used over and over again for forecasts prepared during the life of the mortgage. An amortization table can also be prepared manually, as shown in Table 3-8.

Table 3-9
Loan Progress Chart
Showing Dollar Balance Remaining on a $1000 loan at 12%

Age of Loan	Original Term in Years										
	5	8	10	12	15	16	17	18	19	20	21
1	845	921	945	960	975	978	981	983	985	987	989
2	670	831	883	915	946	953	959	964	969	973	976
3	473	731	813	865	914	925	935	943	950	956	962
4	250	617	734	808	877	894	907	919	929	938	946
5		489	645	744	837	858	877	892	906	917	928
6		345	545	672	790	818	842	862	879	894	907
7		183	432	590	738	773	802	828	849	868	884
8			305	499	680	722	758	789	815	838	858
9			161	395	614	665	708	745	777	805	829
10				279	540	600	652	696	735	767	796
11				148	456	528	589	641	686	725	759
12					361	446	518	579	632	677	717
13					255	353	437	509	571	624	670
14					135	249	347	430	501	563	617
15						132	245	341	424	495	557
16							130	240	336	418	489
17								127	237	332	413
18									126	234	328
19										124	231
20											123

Age of Loan	Original Term in Years										
	22	23	24	25	26	27	28	29	30	35	40
1	990	991	992	993	994	995	995	996	996	998	999
2	979	982	984	986	987	989	990	991	992	996	998
3	966	970	974	977	980	982	984	986	988	993	996
4	952	958	963	967	971	975	978	980	982	990	995
5	936	944	951	957	962	966	970	974	977	987	993
6	918	928	937	944	951	957	962	966	970	984	991
7	898	910	921	930	939	946	952	958	963	980	989
8	875	890	903	915	925	934	941	948	954	975	986
9	850	868	884	897	909	920	929	938	945	970	984
10	821	842	861	878	892	905	916	926	934	964	980
11	788	814	836	855	872	887	900	912	922	958	977
12	751	781	807	830	850	868	883	897	909	950	973
13	710	745	775	802	825	846	864	880	894	942	968
14	663	704	739	770	797	821	842	860	876	933	963
15	611	657	698	734	765	793	817	838	857	922	958
16	551	605	652	694	730	761	789	814	835	910	951
17	485	547	601	648	689	726	758	786	811	897	944
18	409	480	542	597	644	686	723	755	783	882	936
19	325	406	477	539	593	641	683	720	752	865	926

Table 3-9 (cont.)

Age of Loan	Original Term in Years										
	5	8	10	12	15	16	17	18	19	20	21
20	229	322	403	473	536	590	638	680	717	846	916
21	121	227	319	400	471	533	587	635	677	825	904
22		120	225	317	398	468	530	585	633	800	891
23			119	224	315	395	466	528	583	773	876
24				119	222	314	394	464	526	742	859
25					118	221	312	392	462	708	840
26						117	220	311	391	669	819
27							117	219	310	625	795
28								116	219	575	768
29									116	519	737
30										457	703
31										386	664
32										306	621
33										216	571
34										114	516
35											453

Another shortcut for allocating principal and interest is the "Loan Progress Chart," shown in Table 3-9. This chart for a 25-year, 12% loan shows the balance of a $1,000 loan at one-year intervals throughout its life. Let us assume that our mortgage is four years old at the beginning of our forecast period. In order to determine the principal amount paid in the forecast period, we would merely subtract the balance after five years from the previous balance after four years, as follows:

Balance after 4 years—$1,000 loan	$967
Balance after 5 years—$1,000 loan	(957)
Principal payments during forecast period	$ 10

Since our $1,500,000 loan is 1,500 times the size of a $1,000 loan, we merely multiply by 1,500 to find out the principal amortization on our loan.

Principal payments during fourth year for $1,000 loan	$ 10
No. of times greater	✕ 1,500
Principal payments during fourth year for $1,500,000 loan	$15,000

Since total payments on our loan for the year are $189,576, principal would be $15,000, as calculated above, and interest would be $174,576 ($189,576 − $15,000), only $1,398 different from our detailed amortization table.

The above example assumes that our loan is exactly four years old. Rarely, however, are we fortunate enough to have loans which coincide with our forecast period. Therefore, it is necessary to interpolate. Let's assume our loan is five years and five months old at the end of our forecast period. The following calculations would be made:

Balance after 4 years	$967	
Amortization for 5 months (967		
− 957 = 10 × ⁵⁄₁₂)	4	971
Balance after 5 years	$957	
Amortization for 5 months (957		
− 944 = 13 × ⁵⁄₁₂)	5	962
Principal payments during forecast		
period		$ 9

Total principal received during the forecast period would then be $13,500 ($9 × 1,500) and interest would be $176,076 ($189,576 − 13,500).

YIELDS

Up to this point, we have dealt basically with "knowns"; for example:

• Interest rates were fixed at date of purchases.
• All obligations were held to maturity and therefore paid off at par.
• No obligations were purchased during the forecast period.

When we get to the sensitivity portion of our forecast, we will want the flexibility to buy and sell obligations throughout the forecast period. Before attempting to forecast future values of money market instruments, a brief review of the concept of yields is in order. Basically, money market instruments are sold to yield a specific market rate. Thus, if the current market rate for a top-rated corporate bond with a three-year maturity is 12%, no one would pay face for a General Motors bond maturing in three years with a 6% coupon. (The GM bond may have been issued 10 years ago when 6% was a market rate of return on such a bond.) Therefore, someone who wished to earn 12% on this investment would not pay the face amount for a 6% bond, but instead would either not purchase the bond or would expect to pay less than face. Thus, if we could determine what a specific obligation would yield in the open market at any point in time, we would easily calculate its value.

Let's assume we knew we would be required to sell our ABC Corp. bond in two years when market rates for this type of investment would be 12½% in order to pay for capital improvements. It would be essential to our cash flow projections to be able to determine what this particular bond could be sold for at the time we needed these funds. In order to value our bond at some point in the future, we must first determine the length of time it will be outstanding from that specific point until its final maturity. For our example, let's say the period from the disposition of the ABC Corp. bond to final maturity is 14½ years. If we were to look at the components of this bond's cash flow, it would break down as follows:

- $18,125 every 6 months for 29 periods ($500,000 × 7¼% × 6/12)
- $500,000 at maturity in 14½ years

We would then value the above cash stream, using compound financial tables (compounded semiannually), as follows:

Cash Stream	Number of Periods	Value Factor Based on 12½%	Value
$18,125	29	13.2421	$240,013
500,000	29th period	.1724	86,200
			$326,213

Based on the above calculation, MBL will lose $173,787 ($500,000 − $326,213) on the disposal of the ABC Corp. 7¼% bond in order to finance its capital improvements in two years. This illustration vividly points out the need for financial planners to time cash flows to their business needs. If MBL's financial planners had bought a debenture maturing in two years, that debenture would in fact pay off at $500,000. There would have been no need to prematurely dispose of the ABC Corp. bond in an unfavorable rate environment, and consequently lose $173,787. If this seems unrealistic or "too big a loss," it should be noted that on the date this chapter was written, General Motors 7¼% debentures due in 1995 were selling at $65. This means that if $500,000 were sold in today's market, only $325,000 would be realized ($500,000 × 0.65).

The above valuation technique can be used to project cash values of any money market obligation merely by adjusting the number of periods and yield rate.

Estimating Future Rates

The main problem in projecting yields is selecting the right rate. An investment banker once jokingly offered $1 million to anyone who could tell him what rates would be in effect one year from then. Needless to say, forecasting rate environments is extremely difficult. However, the more you know about the factors that affect rates, the better chance you have of projecting them, at least in the short run, with some degree of accuracy.

The rates that a company will receive on market instruments, or will pay on debt, are a function of the following three external factors:

1. *Prime rate.* This is the rate that banks will charge their prime or most creditworthy customers.
2. *Federal discount rate.* This is the rate that the Federal Reserve Bank will charge member banks who borrow money.
3. *Money supply.* The more money that is available, the less it costs to borrow it. The Federal Reserve regulates the amount of money available by changing the discount rate.

These three factors should be considered when estimating future rates. In addition, it should be noted that there is a relationship between the rates earned on various money market instruments. If rates decline on CDs, they will also decline on bonds, Treasury bills, commercial paper, and other money market instruments. Table 3-10 shows yields on several money market instruments at varying dates in 1979 and 1980. The dates and rates themselves are irrelevant and are only presented to show the interrelationship among such instruments.

This interrelationship of money market instruments is best illustrated in Figure 3-1.

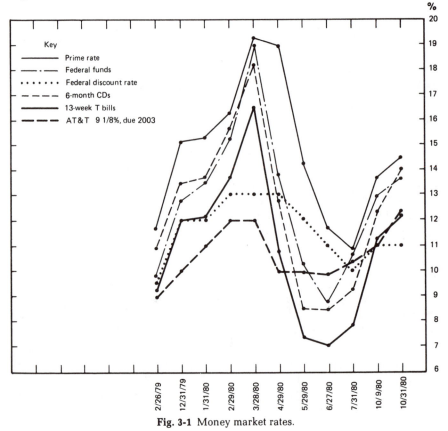

Fig. 3-1 Money market rates.

GENERAL CONCLUSIONS

From Table 3-10 and Figure 3-1, the following conclusions can be drawn:

1. High-grade corporate bonds are the least sensitive to rate fluctuations. During the periods shown, AT&T fluctuated only 3.1 points and PGE fluctuated 5.4 points while the prime rate, the one-month CD rate, and the 13-week T-bill rate fluctuated 8.75, 8.1, and 9.455 points respectively.
2. Commercial paper rates tend to be slightly higher than the CD rates.
3. Treasury bill rates are usually lower than comparable CD or commercial paper rates.
4. The largest gap between the prime rate and other money market rates occurs in a declining rate environment. This indicates a time lag between decreases in money market rates and the prime rate.
5. In a rising rate environment, CD rates tend to be higher than the Federal Funds rate, while in a declining rate environment they tend to be lower.
6. All rates tend to increase and decrease in proportion to each other.

We still have not answered the question as to how to forecast rates. Since it is very difficult to predict rates, the best forecasting advice is to use the most conservative rates: low rates on income-producing securities and high rates on debt obligations. Then adjust them in the sensitivity analysis (see Chapter 9). When estimating your "conservative" forecast rate, the following sources are often helpful.

1. *Current rate environment.* If rates are increasing and we are preparing a short-term forecast, consideration should be given to using higher rates in the forecast.

2. *Predetermined minimum and maximum levels.* There are certain "thresholds of pain" over which prolonged rate levels cannot exist. Therefore it would be unrealistic if we were to project sustained CD rates in the 15 to 20% range for a long-range forecast.

3. *Current inflation rates.* The cost of money, like other costs, tends to rise in periods of increasing inflation and to decrease as inflation rates decline.

4. *Federal policy.* As discussed earlier in this chapter, money market rates tend to rise and fall in conjunction with each other. Consequently, if the Fed is projecting tighter money supply and increasing the discount and Federal Funds rates, it is "safe" to forecast rising CD, commercial paper, and other money market instrument rates.

5. *Bank policy.* Since prime rates and CD rates are set by banks, often

Table 3-10
Yields on Several Money Market Instruments
at Varying Dates in 1979 and 1980

	10/31/80	10/9/80	7/31/80	6/27/80	5/29/80	4/29/80	3/28/80	2/29/80	1/31/80	12/31/79	2/26/79
Prime rate	14½	13½–14	10¾–11	11½–12	14–14½	18½–19½	19¼–19½	16¼–16½	15¼	15–15¼	11½–11¾
Federal Funds	13¼–14	12¼–13½	9½–11	9–9⅜	9¾–11	13–14⅜	18–20	16–14¾	14–13	11½–14	10¼–9 15/16
Federal discount rate	11	11	10	11	12	13	13	13	12	12	9½
Commercial paper:											
30 days	13⅝	12½	8⅞	8⅝	8¾	13⅜	16¾	14½	13¼	13.65	9.80
60 days	13½	12½	8¾	8½	8¾	13¼	16⅞	14½	13.30	13.70	9.95
90 days	13⅝	12½	8.65	8⅜	8	13⅛	17¼	14⅜	13.35	13.70	10.05
Certificates of deposit:											
1 month	13¼	11¾	8.70	8¼	8⅛	13	16¼	14½	13	13	9⅝
2 months	13½	12⅛	8½	8¼	8.20	13	16½	14⅝	13.2	13¼	10⅛
3 months	14.05	12⅜	8½	8⅜	8.30	12¾	17⅝	15	13¼	13⅛	10¼
6 months	14.15	12.45	9.20	8½	8½	12¾	18.15	15.6	13⅝	13.50	10.85
1 year	13⅞	12⅜	8¾	8	8	12	17¼	15¼	13⅛	12⅛	10¼
Treasury bills:											
13 weeks	12.331	11.295	8.221	7.077	7.675	10.788	16.532	13.7	12.038	12.105	9.293
26 weeks	12.284	11.140	8.276	7.108	7.753	10.790	15.700	13.629	11.846	11.880	9.370
AT&T 7⅛% due 2003	12.431	11	*	9.7	10	10	12	12	11	10	8.9
PGE 8% due 2003	13	13	*	10	*	12	*	13	13	11	9.6
PGE 8⅜% due 2002	13	*	*	*	11		13	15	12	12	9.6

*Price not quoted

discussions with bankers from whom the company borrows will disclose rate trends.

6. *Investment bankers' policy.* Most investment bankers are heavily involved in money market instruments. Therefore, discussions with them may also disclose rate trends.

7. *Rates on new corporate and municipal bonds.* Major corporations, like Ford, GM, etc., have vast resources to study the market prior to issuing new debt. As a result, their rates are often indicative of future rate trends. For example, if these companies are issuing new debt at higher rates, it might be an indication that they feel rates will go even higher. Moreover, if a major corporation stops issuing debt in a high rate environment, it may be an indication that a "threshold of pain" has been reached and rates may tend to decline.

Exhibit 3-1
MBL Mfg. Co.
Forecasting Worksheet for the Year Ended 12/31/19X1

| | Cash Flow | | Income Statement | Balance Sheet | | | | | | |
	Principal	Interest	Interest Income	Cash	Savings Account	Short-Term Investments	Long-Term Investments	Unamortized Discount	Accrued Interest Received	Retained Earnings
Certificates of deposit	$ 25,000	$ 3,063	$ 2,866	$ 28,063		$(25,000)			$2,866 (3,063)	$ 2,866
Savings accounts	2,000		729	2,000	$(2,000) 729					729
Treasury bills	35,000		979	35,000		(35,000)		$ 979		979
Municipal and corporate bonds	300,000	63,250	63,250 750	363,250			$(300,000)	750		63,250 750
Self-amortizing obligations	16,398	173,178	173,178	189,576			(16,398)			173,178
	$378,398	$239,491	$241,752	$617,889	$1,271	$(60,000)	$(316,398)	$1,729	$ (197)	$241,752

4

Inventories

Inventory, like sales, does not directly affect cash. Nor do changes in inventory levels directly affect cash. The mere utilization of inventory in production does not require a cash outlay. If it costs $1,000 to produce one widget and we sell 100 widgets, cash outflow is *not* $100,000. Cash is affected only by purchases of raw materials.

Factors Affecting Inventory Purchases

In projecting the cash outflows required for purchases of inventory, the following factors should be considered.

1. *Sales growth.* Although not necessarily directly related to production, if we intend to increase sales, we will have to increase production. This increased production will, at some point in time, require inventory purchases.

2. *Plans for expansion.* This goes hand in hand with sales growth. If the company expects to expand into new sales areas, this will translate into increased production and, correspondingly, increased inventory purchases.

3. *Production capacity.* At times, sales and marketing personnel project sales growth in terms of ability to produce an infinite amount of product. As a practical matter, there is only a finite number of goods that can be produced within the physical constraints of existing equipment and manpower. When converting increased sales into increased production, we must be sure that we do not exceed these levels of reality. If we do, either sales figures will have to be adjusted or new equipment, etc., will have to be obtained and its cost factored into the cash flow forecast. (See Chapter 9, "Cash Flow Sensitivity.")

4. *Production lag time.* Some products may require years of production prior to completion and subsequent sale. Throughout manufacturing of these products, inventory must be purchased and put into production without a related sale. This time lag may therefore impact several forecast periods.

5. *Safety stock requirements.* Many companies require minimum levels of inventory to be on hand at all times, regardless of sales, in order to ensure "continuous" production. These requirements must be added to the actual purchase needs of the company.

6. *Economic order quantities (EOQ).* Based on discounts available, costs to ship, warehouse costs, etc., it is more economical to order specific quantities of certain goods. Therefore, more material purchases (i.e., EOQ) may be forecasted than the actual material needs.

7. *Availability of funds.* The proper timing of purchases with otherwise idle funds is one way of minimizing the cost of money. For example, if collections on accounts receivable are stable throughout the year but the company is required to make semiannual debt payments on its outstanding debentures, purchases of inventory at the same time might require incremental bank borrowings at high costs. Countercyclical inventory purchases, on the other hand, may incur only nominal warehousing costs, thus reducing total operating costs for the company.

8. *Seasonality of industry.* Certain products—for example, artificial Christmas trees, swimming pools, fall fashions, etc.—are traditionally sold at specific times during the year. However, their production may be continuous throughout the period.

9. *Order time.* Certain raw materials, packaging, etc., may require long order periods if they are difficult to obtain, or if they are custom-made. For example, a builder can be fairly certain that studs, plywood, nails, etc. will be easily obtainable when and as the need for them arises. However, a hand-carved Italian marble fireplace mantel may require months to order and must be on hand before a home requiring it may be completed.

Production Scheduling Reports

In order to properly forecast cash flows for inventory purposes, it is necessary to obtain or prepare detailed production scheduling reports. For illustrative purposes, we will generate some simple schedules as part of the forecasting package. However, in reality, many companies will already have available detailed production schedules that can be incorporated into the cash flow forecast.

The following schedules should be prepared for each component of inventory that must be purchased from outside vendors. Remember that in preparing the forecast, we are *not* preparing "Work in Process" costing schedules. Therefore, we are not concerned with overhead charges normally added in production costing systems. Instead, we are concerned with determining the latest possible date that we can purchase a single component required in the production process.

The first step in preparing a scheduling report is to determine when a specific part will be needed (i.e., put into production). Next, we must determine if the goods to be used are already in inventory. If they are, it is unnecessary to include them in our scheduling reports since no inventory purchase is required. We must, however, remember that for scheduling purposes, existing inventory should never be reduced below safety stock requirements.

We should begin the scheduling report by obtaining a list of the type and quantity of raw materials that must be *purchased* for the manufacture of each unit. Bob Burkheart, our production manager, has supplied us with the following parts list for the A-40623 Home Window air-conditioning unit:

Part Number	Name	Unit of Measurement	Quantity
B-4063	Wing screw	ea.	16
B-40624	¼ inch screw	ea.	10
B-4065	½ inch screw	ea.	5
A-3264	4 × 8-aluminum sheet	ea.	3
C-4803	Condenser	ea.	1
00064	¼ inch brass pipe	ft.	12′

Our next step is to prepare a time chart of expected production dates for the air-conditioning unit. This schedule should take into consideration past production output adjusted for projected sales growth. In projecting production to meet sales growth, we must be sure to factor in the production required to replace defective returned merchandise. For example, if in 19X0, we produced 1,000 units, had a 10% return rate for defective merchandise, and projected a 2¾% production increase due to sales growth, then production would have to be increased by 3% in 19X1 as follows:

No. of units produced in previous year	1,000
Projected growth rate	2.75%
Required production increase due to sales growth	27 units
Required production increase due to sales growth	27
Production required, including factor for defective merchandise	110%
Actual total production increase required	29.7 (say 30)

$$\frac{\text{Actual total production increase required}}{\text{No. of units produced in previous year}} = \frac{30}{1,000} = 3\%$$

Table 4-1
MBL Mfg. Co.
Expected Production Start Dates for A.C. Unit 40623

Date	19X0 Quantity	Estimated Average Productivity Increase to Meet Sales Growth	19X1 Quantity
January 1, 19X0	1,000	3%	1,030
February 1	1,000		1,030
March 10	4,000		4,120
April 10	4,000		4,120
May 15	4,000		4,120
June	-0-		—
July 1	2,500		2,575
August 1	2,500		2,575
September 10	2,500		2,575
October 10	1,500		1,545
November 5	1,000		1,030
December 1	2,000		2,060
January 1, 19X1	1,030		1,061

The time chart shown in Table 4-1 was prepared for estimating a production timetable for unit 40823.

For illustrative purposes, we have assumed uneven production throughout the year. For example, the factory may be shut down annually in June for vacations or retooling of machines. In addition, extra help may be put on to increase production to meet peak demands in the months of March through May.

Although a production scheduling report should be prepared for each component to be purchased, for illustrative purposes we shall prepare a sample report only for the B-4063 wing screw. Remember that the purpose of this schedule is to determine the *latest* date on which materials must be available to meet the production schedule. Keep in mind that there may be more than one start date each month. In fact, certain products have various start dates throughout the month. If this is the case, the production schedule either can be expanded to include each date or can use an average start date. Table 4-2 is a sample of a production scheduling report.

In preparing the previous two schedules, several factors should be kept in mind:

1. We are concerned only with the required start date for the wing screw. Therefore, if we begin with the start date of the entire unit, we must factor in the number of days before the wing screw is needed. In our example, although production is started on an air conditioner on January 1, the wing screw would not be needed until January 11. Remember that this time lag may be extremely significant in a long production cycle.

2. The mere fact that a part has been purchased and is in inventory doesn't mean you have immediate access to it. For example, requisition and delivery from a central warehouse may be required. In our example, a wing screw needed on January 11 would have to be ordered from the warehouse on January 9 in order to allow for the required two-day delivery time.

3. If a part is needed on a certain day we must make sure it is ordered sufficiently in advance of the required delivery date. In our example, if we needed the wing screw in the warehouse on January 9, the order should have been placed on December 26 to allow for a two-week delivery period.

4. Be sure to calculate the total part quantity needed for each unit of production. For example, we will need 16,480 wing screws to manufacture the 1,030 air conditioners scheduled for January's production since each unit requires 16 wing screws.

Now that the production scheduling has been completed, we must adjust the calculated production requirements for economic order quantity and safety stock.

Economic Order Quantity

The individual who is responsible for inventory purchases has probably already calculated the most economical quantities to order of each inventory component. However, it is a good idea to recheck the calculations and

Table 4-2
MBL Mfg. Co.
Production Scheduling Report B-4063 Wing Screw

A.C. Unit 40263 Start Date	Add Number of Production Days Before B-4063 Is Needed	Deduct Number of Delivery Days from Warehouse to Production Site
January 1	10	2
February 1		
March 10		
April 10		
May 15		
July 1		
August 1		
September 10		
October 20		
November 5		
December 1		
January		

assumptions. If the EOQ hasn't already been calculated, then a calculation must be made, accompanied by a recommendation that consideration should be given to ordering parts in that quantity. This recommendation is just one of the side benefits a company obtains from a cash flow forecast, a fresh perspective on the money management policies. Inappropriate order quantities can often increase inventory and shipping costs, reduce discounts taken, etc., all of which decrease a company's cash flow and profits.

Since savings on bulk orders are often offset by higher inventory carrying costs, and smaller, more frequent orders often require increased processing and handling costs, the key money management question is when and how much inventory should be purchased.

Let's assume MBL has ascertained the following information:

Total number of wing screws required in 19X1 (428,976 ÷ 12)	35,748 dozen
Cost per dozen	$1.60
Processing cost per order	5.00
Warehousing and carrying costs (% of average inventory value)	5%

Given the information presented in Table 4-2, you could manually calculate the most cost-effective order quantity by selecting various quan-

Deduct Number of Delivery Days from Order Date to Warehouse Receipt	Order Date for B-4063	Quantity Needed
14	Dec. 26	16,480 (1030 × 16)
	Jan. 26	16,480 (1030 × 16)
	Mar. 4	65,920 (4120 × 16)
	Apr. 4	65,920 (4120 × 16)
	May 9	65,920 (4120 × 16)
	June 25	41,200 (2575 × 16)
	July 26	41,200 (2575 × 16)
	Sept. 4	41,200 (2575 × 16)
	Oct. 14	24,720 (1545 × 16)
	Oct. 30	16,480 (1030 × 16)
	Nov. 25	32,960 (2060 × 16)
	Dec. 26	16,976 (1061 × 16)
Total for 19X1 (Jan. 26–Dec. 26)		428,976

tities at random and costing them out. This could be done as follows:

MBL Mfg. Co.
Calculation of Order and Processing Costs Per Order Quantity

Order size	100	1,000	5,000	10,000	17,874	35,748
Number of orders required	357	36	8	4	2	1
Avg. inventory (order size ÷ 2)	50	500	2,500	5,000	8,937	17,874
Avg. inventory cost (avg. inv. × $1.60)	$ 80	800	4,000	8,000	14,299	28,598
Carrying cost (avg. inv. cost × 5%)	$ 4	40	200	400	715	1,430
Processing costs (Number of orders × $5.00)	$1,785	180	40	20	10	5
	$1,789	220	240	420	725	1,435

Of the possible order quantities considered above, the most economical is a 1,000-unit order. However, we do not know if there is still a more economical order quantity between 1,000 and 5,000. We could prepare additional calculations for various quantities between 1,000 and 5,000. But an easier alternative is to use the economic order quantity formula:

$$\text{Economic order quantity} = \frac{2 \times \text{annual required units} \times \text{cost per order}}{\text{Cost per unit} \times \text{carrying cost}}$$

$$\text{EOQ} = \sqrt{\frac{2 \times 35{,}748 \times \$5}{\$1.60 \times 5\%}}$$

$$= \sqrt{\frac{357{,}480}{.08}}$$

$$= \sqrt{4{,}468{,}500}$$

$$= 2{,}114$$

Therefore, the most economical quantity for MBL is 2,114 dozen or 25,368 screws.

Safety Stock

Unfortunately, our productivity scheduling report is based on assumptions that may or may not hold up. For example, increased productivity on the air-conditioning unit may mean that the date the wing screw is needed has been accelerated. In addition, vendor delays or shipping delays may cause increased delivery time. Such conditions may give rise to a stock-out. If wing screws are not available on schedule, production may have to be halted and machines and personnel may remain idle or operate at less than peak efficiency. Both of these conditions will cost the company money. Therefore, no company will knowingly schedule inventory usage down below a certain safety level. Instead, companies will allow a sufficient amount of excess inventory in order to guard against errors and unexpected problems.

Excess inventory calculations and safety stock levels are normally maintained by a company. Again, it is a good idea to review the company policy and recalculate the safety levels. The most effective way to do this is to compare prior years' inventory usage forecasts to actual usage and to determine the variance. Table 4-3 shows the schedule that can then be prepared using MBL's 19X0 historical results.

The next step in calculating safety levels is to divide the deviation squared by the number of months and then calculate the square root. Since MBL has no production during the month of June, this month is eliminated. Thus:

$$\sqrt{\frac{10{,}926{,}600}{11}} = \sqrt{993{,}327.27} = 996.66$$

Table 4-3
MBL Mfg. Co.
*Calculation of Deviation Squared on Historical Inventory
Usage*

Month	Units Put into Production Actual	Forecast	Deviation Actual vs. Forecast	Squared
January	16,000	16,840	+ 840	705,600
February	16,000	16,300	+ 300	90,000
March	64,000	63,400	− 600	360,000
April	64,000	63,280	− 720	518,400
May	64,000	65,100	+ 1,100	1,210,000
June	-0-	-0-	-0-	-0-
July	40,000	40,370	+ 370	136,900
August	40,000	40,280	+ 280	78,400
September	40,000	37,680	− 2,320	5,382,400
October	24,000	23,400	− 600	360,000
November	16,000	15,800	− 200	40,000
December	32,000	33,430	+ 1,430	2,044,900
				10,926,600

Mathematically, if we double this number (996.66 × 2 = 1,993), and use 1,993 as our safety stock quantity, we are 95% confident that we will not have a stock-out. If we triple the number (996.66 × 3 = 2,990), a safety stock quantity of 2,990 will yield a 99% confidence level of not having a stock-out.

Inventory Purchase Prices

Now that we have calculated the required production quantities, we must price our inventory needs. Prices of goods to be purchased throughout the forecast period will fluctuate based on the economic environment at the time of purchase. Therefore it is necessary to examine the following sources in order to price future inventory purchases.

1. *Invoices.* One of the best starting points for forecasting inventory price is the current price. A review of the latest invoices will indicate the amount the company is currently paying for the part. A review of the latest invoice paid by MBL indicates that the company is paying $1.60 per dozen for the B-4063 wing screw.

2. *Price lists.* Many vendors supply the purchasing department with standard price lists. These lists often indicate that a specific price is good through a certain date. If this is the case, we will know the prevailing price for part of our forecast period and we will have some idea of when we can expect a price change.

3. *Supply contracts.* Companies often sign contracts to supply specified goods for a specified time at a fixed price. Again, if this is the case, we will know the current price for a specific period.

4. *Conversation with vendors.* Vendors often produce revised price lists in advance of the effective date or have programmed price increases within their projections. Although some vendors are hesitant to quote future prices, others are more than willing to indicate the magnitude of such increases, especially to larger customers.

5. *Industry statistics.* Many industries have trade publications that not only review past statistics but also indicate expected future price trends.

6. *Related industry activity.* There is, for example, a direct correlation between the increase in steel prices and the increase in the cost of steel screws. Knowledge of this correlation, coupled with past history on the time lag between increased steel prices and increased wing screw prices, may give us an indication of future price increases.

7. *Inflation.* Like everything else, the price of wing screws will increase as inflation rises. Therefore, if economists are projecting increased inflation, this can be translated into increased wing screw prices.

Purchasing Schedules

Per discussion with Jim Burton, purchasing manager, you have learned that although MBL is currently paying $1.60 per dozen for the B-4063 wing screw, the price will be increased to $1.75 per dozen the first of the year. The new price will be in effect through June 15, 19X1. Jim also indicated that if inflation continues at the current 12% rate, there will be at least a 15% price increase in June. Therefore, the price will be further increased to $2.01 per dozen ($1.75 × 115%) on June 16.

We have also learned that after the 16,480 wing screws were put into production on December 16, 19X0, there were 103,000 wing screws in inventory.

We are now ready to forecast inventory purchases. This can be accomplished by use of a purchasing schedule, as shown in Table 4-4. Production requirements will be posted to the schedule until a negative balance is reached. At that point purchases must be made in order to reach a positive balance. By reflecting the safety stock requirement as the first production requirement, we automatically ensure that it is never used in pro-

Table 4-4
MBL Mfg. Co.
Purchasing Schedule for Wing Screws

	Purchases	Amounts Put in Production	Balance	Price per Dozen	Total Cash Outflow
Balance 1/1/19X1			103,000		
Amt. of safety stock required		(2,990)	100,010		
Amt. needed					
Jan. 26, 19XX		(16,480)	83,530		
March 4		(65,920)	17,610		
April 4		(65,920)	(48,310)		
Required purchases prior to April 4	25,368		(22,942)	$1.75	$ 3,670
	25,368		2,426	1.75	3,670
Amt. needed May 9		(65,920)	(63,494)		
Required purchases prior to May 9	25,368		(38,126)	1.75	3,670
	25,368		(12,758)	1.75	3,670
	25,368		12,610	1.75	3,670
Amt. needed June 25		(41,200)	(28,590)		
Required purchases prior to June 25	25,368		(3,222)	2.01	4,249
	25,368		22,146	2.01	4,249
Amt. needed July 26		(41,200)	(19,054)		
Required purchases prior to July 26	25,368		6,314	2.01	4,249
Amt. needed Sept. 4		(41,200)	(34,886)		
Required purchase prior to Sept. 4	25,368		(9,518)	2.01	4,249
	25,368		15,850	2.01	4,249
Amt. needed Oct. 14		(24,720)	(8,870)		
Required purchases prior to Oct. 30	25,368		16,498	2.01	4,249
Amt. needed Oct. 30		(16,480)	18		
Amt. needed Nov. 25		(32,960)	(32,942)		
Required purchases prior to Nov. 25	25,368		(7,574)	2.01	4,249
	25,368		17,794	2.01	4,249
Amt. needed Dec. 26		(16,976)	818		
					$52,342

duction. The schedule shown in Table 4-4 is designed to summarize monthly purchase requirements in order to facilitate a monthly cash flow forecast. Since MBL is preparing an annual cash flow forecast, this schedule can be simplified as follows.

MBL Mfg. Co.
Purchasing Schedule for Wing Screws

	Purchases	Amounts Put into Production	Balance
Balance 1/1/19X1			103,000
Amt. of safety stock required		(2,990)	100,010
Amt. needed during year		(428,976)	(328,966)
Required purchases (25,368 × 13)	329,784		818

We could then price out the 329,784 purchases using an average price of $1.88 ($1.75 + 2.01 = 3.76 ÷ 2 = $1.88) as follows:

Total number of wing screws purchased	329,784
÷ 12 to obtain number of dozen	÷ 12
	27,482
× average price per dozen	× $ 1.88
	$51,666

The difference between the monthly calculation and the average annual calculation is only $676 ($52,342 − 51,666). Since the difference is not material, we can use either calculation.

When and How Inventory Is to Be Purchased

We have just determined when inventory must be ordered. However, the mere placing of a purchase order does not require a cash outflow. In order to forecast cash outflows, we must determine when and how inventory is to be paid.

WHEN

Vendors often offer terms on their sales. For example, we may be entitled to a 2% discount if we pay within 10 days. If not, payment may be due within 30 days. Therefore, we must evaluate the discount, as we did in Chapter 2, and compare it to our cost of money to determine if we should avail ourselves of the discount.

HOW

Certain vendors often provide financing for their purchases. That is, the purchase may be paid for in installations with the unpaid balance bearing interest at a stated rate. For purposes of cash flow forecasting, such purchases should be reduced from total inventory purchases and treated as debt. (See Chapter 6 for forecasting debt.)

Inventory Purchase Payment Schedules

For illustrative purposes, let's assume that through August 15th, based on MBL's borrowing costs, it makes sense to take advantage of the 2% discount and pay on the 10th day. Thereafter, no discount will be taken and invoices will be paid on the 30th day. Our payment schedule will then look like that shown in Table 4-5.

Table 4-5
MBL Mfg. Co.
Inventory Purchase Payment Schedule

Date Ordered	Cost	Discount Taken	Payment Date	19X1 Payment
April 3	7,340	2%	April 13	7,193 (7,340 × 98%)
May 9	11,010	2%	May 19	10,790 (11,010 × 98%)
June 25	8,498	2%	July 5	8,328 (8,498 × 98%)
July 26	4,249	2%	Aug. 5	4,164 (4,249 × 98%)
Sept. 4	8,498	—	Oct. 4	8,498
Oct 30.	4,249	—	Nov. 29	4,249
Nov. 25	8,498	—	Dec. 25	8,498
				$51,720

We can now post the $51,720 cash purchases of the wing screw to the forecast worksheet (Exhibit 4-1).

In addition to the $51,720 purchase, we must add order costs of $65 (13 orders × $5 per order). Let's also assume, for illustrative purposes, that inventory purchases for the remaining components of the air-conditioning units total $800,000 and that $300,000 of this amount will be paid in cash with the balance being financed. Beginning December 31, 19X1, the $500,000 is to be repaid in five equal semiannual installments of $100,000, with the outstanding balance accruing interest at 13%. The accrued interest is to be paid at maturity. These items can also be posted to our forecasting worksheet. The remaining $500,000 will be posted as a liability and will be dealt with in Chapter 6, "Debt."

Balance Sheet and Income Statement Effects

Although we have posted the cash outflows related to inventory purchases, we have also been asked to prepare an income statement and balance sheet. Therefore, we must calculate the income effect of inventory.
Since inventory is charged to income in the form of cost of goods sold only
when sales are made, costs of sales can be determined by multiplying total
number of sales units forecasted by the average cost per unit.

Remember that cost of goods sold includes not only the costs of raw
materials but also labor and factory overhead. Let's assume that the total
unit cost is $37.50 broken down as follows:

Material	$20.60
Labor	10.00
Overhead	6.90
	$37.50

We can therefore calculate cost of goods sold for balance sheet and
income statement purposes as follows:

Total projected sales units (per Chapter 2)	26,775
× cost per unit	× $ 37.50
	$1,004,063

By posting the $1,004,063 to the forecasting worksheet as a reduction of
inventory, we will obtain a negative inventory balance. This is due to the
fact that so far we have only charged material to inventory. In Chapter 7,
"Other Areas to be Forecasted," we will see payroll and other overhead
costs being added to inventory.

Obsolete Inventory

So far we have discussed only the costs associated with the purchases of
inventory to be put into production. However, old and obsolete inventory
can be both a cost and a source of cash. Since obsolete inventory must be
warehoused, counted, etc., there are indirect costs that could be saved by
eliminating it. In addition, if the inventory is of no use to the company, its
sale may provide some additional revenues. Any expected cash from the
sale of old or obsolete inventory should be included in the cash flow
forecast.

Exhibit 4-1
MBL Mfg. Co.
Forecasting Worksheet for the Year Ended 12/31/19X1

	Cash Flow	Income Statement	Balance Sheet			
	Inventory	Cost of Goods Sold	Cash	Inventory	Accounts Payable	Retained Earnings
Purchase B-4063 wing screw	$ (51,720)		$ (51,720)	$ 51,720		
Order costs	(65)		(65)	65		
Other purchases	(300,000)		(300,000)	300,000	$500,000	
Cost of goods sold		$(1,004,063)		(1,004,063)		$(1,004,063)
	$(351,785)	$(1,004,063)	$(351,785)	$(152,278)	$500,000	$(1,004,063)

Property, Plant, and Equipment

Cash flow is impacted by two aspects of property, plant, and equipment:

1. Costs related to existing property, plant, and equipment
2. Costs related to expected acquisitions of property, plant, and equipment during the forecast period

The cash outflows associated with these two areas can be further subdivided into the following two categories:

1. Costs associated with *owned* property plant and equipment
2. Costs associated with *leased* property plant and equipment

Let's now examine each of these areas individually.

Costs Related to Existing Owned Property, Plant, and Equipment

In order to control all of a company's fixed assets, a checklist for each owned asset should be prepared. This checklist should include a description of possible cost expenditures and a projection of when these expenditures might take place. In general, repairs and maintenance, property taxes, insurance, and depreciation would be the normal types of expenses associated with property, plant, and equipment.

REPAIRS AND MAINTENANCE

In order to forecast repairs and maintenance, it is necessary to estimate both *scheduled* or routine maintenance (protective maintenance) and *unscheduled* repairs of broken or damaged assets.

Scheduled Repairs and Maintenance

The timing of scheduled repairs and maintenance can usually be obtained from the production department. Many factories are shut down for certain periods of time in order to perform major protective maintenance functions. In addition, regular maintenance is often performed at scheduled intervals; for example, after a predetermined number of machine hours. This type of routine maintenance is usually performed by either the company's own maintenance personnel or outside contractors. If the company's own personnel perform the maintenance, their salaries will be forecasted as part of the overall payroll forecast (see Chapter 7). However, any out-of-pocket costs such as the cost of replacement parts must be included in the cash flow forecast in the period in which the maintenance is forecasted to be performed. An alternative to using the company's own "service team" is hiring outside contractors to perform the work. If this is the case, we can usually get a good idea of projected cash outlays by reviewing maintenance contracts.

Through discussions with Bob Burkheart, you have learned that all of MBL's metal bending machines and steel presses are under service contracts with the vendor. The following is a summary of MBL's service contracts with outside vendors.

MBL Mfg. Co.
Summary of Vendor Service Contracts

Vendor	Item Covered	Annual Cost	Payment Dates	Date of Expiration
ABC Co.	Bending machine 1	$6,000	Monthly	Aug. 30, 19X1
ABC Co.	Bending machine 2	6,000	Monthly	Sept. 30, 19X1
ABC Co.	Bending machine 3	8,000	Monthly	Sept. 30, 19X2
XYZ Co.	Steel press 1	3,000	6/30 and 12/31	June 30, 19X1
XYZ Co.	Steel press 2	4,000	1/1	Jan. 1, 19X2

Further discussions with Bob Burkheart reveal that these contracts are expected to be renewed on their expiration dates and that a 10% to 14% increase would not be unusual. Therefore, for forecasting purposes, an average of 12% can be used.

With this information, we are now ready to forecast cash outlays for service contracts by use of the schedule shown in Table 5-1.

Table 5-1

MBL Mfg. Co.

Calculation of Service Contract Payments for 19X1

| | Bending Machines | | | Steel Presses | | |
Month	1	2	3	1	2	Total
January	$500	$500	$667	$—	$4,000	$5,667
February	500	500	667	—	—	1,667
March	500	500	667	—	—	1,667
April	500	500	667	—	—	1,667
May	500	500	667	—	—	1,667
June	500	500	667	1,500	—	3,167
July	500	500	667	—	—	1,667
August	500	500	667	—	—	1,667
September	560	500	667	—	—	1,727
October	560	560	667	—	—	1,787
November	560	560	667	—	—	1,787
December	560	560	667	1,680	—	3,467
						$27,604

The schedule shown in Table 5-1 was prepared to facilitate a monthly cash flow forecast. Since we are preparing an annual cash flow, the calculations could be simplified, as shown in Table 5-2.

The amount obtained in Table 5-2 can now be posted to our forecasting worksheet (Exhibit 5-1). Keep in mind that if we were to prepare a monthly income statement, we would have to accrue a monthly expense for steel presses 1 and 2. For example, although total cash paid in January

Table 5-2

MBL Mfg. Co.

*Simplified Calculation of Service Contract
Payments for 19X1*

Machine	Payment Terms	Amount
Bending machine 1	$500 per month × 8 mo.	$ 4,000
Bending machine 1	$560 per month × 4 mo.	2,240
Bending machine 2	$500 per month × 9 mo.	4,500
Bending machine 2	$560 per month × 3 mo.	1,680
Bending machine 3	$667 per month × 12 mo.	8,000
Steel press 1	$1,500 on June 30	1,500
Steel press 1	$1,500 + 12½% increase	1,680
Steel press 2	$4,000 on Jan. 1	4,000
		$27,600

was $5,667, the January forecasted income statement would reflect maintenance expense on an accrual basis, as follows:

Bending machine 1	$ 500
Bending machine 2	500
Bending machine 3	667
Steel press 1 ($3,180 × 1/12)	265
Steel press 2 ($4,000 × 1/12)	333
	$2,265

Not only does MBL use outside contractors to service its machinery but it has one drill press that it services itself. Maintenance for the drill press is done in June when the factory is shut down for vacations. The following is a work order for the June maintenance:

Job order # 1463	Drill Press Maintenance	
Scheduled date <u>June 15, 19X1</u>		
Job Description	**Hours**	**Quantity**
Replace drill bits 4074	6	24 (ea)
Replace gear shaft 1032	10	2 (ea)
Replace cog wheels 1068	15	32 (ea)
Replace gear springs 2046	5	40 (ea)
Grease gear mechanism	2	1 (qt)
Clean all moving parts	15	—

Since the labor hours will be accounted for in the payroll section of our forecast, it is only necessary to cost out the parts for the above work order, as follows:

MBL Mfg. Co.
Calculation of June Drill Press Maintenance

Item	Quantity	Cost per Unit	Total Cost
Drill bit 4074	24	$ 65	$1,560
Gear shaft 1032	2	450	900
Cog wheel 1068	32	30	960
Gear spring 2046	40	8	320
Grease	1	5	5
			$3,745

We can now post this cost of replacement parts to the forecasting worksheet. Again, if we were preparing a monthly forecast, even though the cash outflow of $3,745 would occur in June, $312 ($3,745 ÷ 12) would have to be allocated as a monthly accounting expense throughout the year and the appropriate accruals and prepaid accounts established.

Unscheduled Repairs and Maintenance

Unscheduled repairs are exactly that: *unscheduled*. Projecting when a machine will break down is virtually impossible. Therefore, forecasting the cash requirement to pay for such repairs is difficult at best. There are, however, several helpful hints that should be considered:

1. The number of times a specific breakdown occurred in the past and the cost to repair.
2. The manufacturer's estimate of the useful lives of the various machine components.
3. The age of a specific machine. Certain machine parts have useful lives dependent on the number of machine hours used.

Let's assume that experience has shown that bending machine drive shafts wear out and must be replaced periodically after approximately 1,600 hours of service. We have also learned that MBL's bending machines are in operation approximately eight hours a day during most of the year. During the peak production months of March through May, they are in use 10 hours a day. In addition, all machines are shut down during the month of June. Let's further assume that the installation of a new drive shaft costs $600 and that MBL's bending machines have been in service the following number of hours since their drive shafts were last replaced:

	Hours
Bending machine 1	1,400
Bending machine 2	200
Bending machine 3	1,200

We could then program the months in which expected repairs will be required by first, calculating the number of production hours in the month, and second, maintaining a running total of machine operating hours. This could be done as shown in Table 5-3.

Note that by the end of January, machine 1 would have been in operation for 1,576 hours. Therefore, after 24 hours of operation in the month of February, it would require a drive shaft replacement. It would then operate 136 hours (160 − 24) in February with the new drive shaft.

One conservative way of providing for unscheduled repairs is to set up an actual cash reserve. A specific amount of cash, perhaps in the form of a CD or savings account, can be physically set aside for this purpose. You will remember from Chapter 3 that MBL maintains a $10,000 CD at all times. Perhaps this CD is used just for such contingencies. If this is the case, this reserve is to be used solely for unscheduled repairs and is not to be forecasted for any other purpose.

Table 5-3

MBL Mfg. Co.

Forecast of Cash Requirements for Repairs During 19X1

Month	Available Machine Hours	Hours × Days	Machine Hours 1	2	3	Repair Cost
Dec. 31, 19X0			1,400	200	1,200	$ —
Jan.	176	(8 × 22)	1,576	376	1,376	—
Feb.	160	(8 × 20)	136	536	1,536	600
Mar.	230	(10 × 23)	366	766	166	600
Apr.	200	(10 × 20)	566	966	366	—
May	230	(10 × 23)	796	1,196	596	—
June	—	—	—	—	—	—
July	168	(8 × 21)	964	1,364	764	—
Aug.	184	(8 × 23)	1,148	1,548	948	—
Sept.	168	(8 × 21)	1,316	116	1,116	600
Oct.	176	(8 × 22)	1,492	292	1,292	—
Nov.	176	(8 × 22)	68	468	1,468	600
Dec.	168	(8 × 21)	236	636	36	600
						$3,000

PROPERTY TAXES

If the company owns its own office building, plant, or warehouse, it is required to pay property taxes. These taxes are usually paid either semi-annually or annually. A starting point in forecasting these taxes is with prior years' tax bills. In addition, most municipalities are willing to give estimates of projected tax payments since the revenue is already a part of their budgets. Let's assume that from discussion with MBL's municipalities, the tax payments shown in Table 5-4 are estimated for 19X1.

For accounting purposes, the tax payments shown in Table 5-4 must be allocated evenly throughout the year. However, for cash flow purposes, they can be summarized and posted to the cash worksheet as shown in Table 5-5.

The schedule shown in Table 5-5 illustrates that certain municipalities may have different tax payment dates for different components of their taxes, even on the same building.

Once this schedule is completed, we can post the tax payments to the forecasting worksheet.

Table 5-4

MBL Mfg. Co.

Schedule of Expected Property Tax Payments by Month for
19X1

Property	Type	Payment Dates	Annual Amount
Plant	School	Dec. 15	$16,400
	County	Dec. 15	8,000
	Water	June 15	2,000
Warehouse 1	City	Jan. 1 and July 1	4,000
	County	Jan. 1 and July 1	3,000
	Sewer	Jan. 1 and July 1	500
Warehouse 2	City	June 30	8,000
	County	June 30	2,000
	Water & Sewer	June 30 and Dec. 30	1,000
			$44,900

Table 5-5

MBL Mfg. Co.

Schedule of Expected Property Tax Payments
by Month for 19X1

Payment Date	Property	Amount of Payment		
January	Warehouse 1	(½ × $4,000)	$2,000	
	Warehouse 1	(½ × $3,000)	1,500	
	Warehouse 1	(½ × $ 500)	250	
				$ 3,750
June	Plant		2,000	
	Warehouse 2		8,000	
	Warehouse 2		2,000	
	Warehouse 2	(½ × $1,000)	500	
				12,500
July	Warehouse 1	(½ × $4,000)	2,000	
	Warehouse 1	(½ × $3,000)	1,500	
	Warehouse 1	(½ × $ 500)	250	
				3,750
December	Plant		16,400	
	Plant		8,000	
	Warehouse 2	(½ × $1,000)	500	
				24,900
				$44,900

INSURANCE

As with property taxes, the best place to start the forecasting process is with a look at past invoices coupled with conversations with the insurance broker. Again, we should prepare a summary of insurance coverage on owned property. In preparing this schedule, we should keep in mind that various insurance companies use different payment schedules and therefore a careful reading of the payment terms under each contract is important. Three of the more typical payment schedules are as follows.

1. *Three-year policy prepaid in advance.* The chief benefit of this policy is that you are protected against price increases during the policy term. However, you must pay for the policy in advance. An evaluation should be made of expected premium increases versus your ability to utilize these funds in your own business. Although three-year terms are the most typical for this type of policy, other periods are available from certain insurance companies.

2. *Three-year policy paid annually.* This type of policy is basically the same as the previous policy. However, since it is paid annually, the insurance company usually adds a finance charge on the unpaid balance. In essence, the insurance company is loaning you the money to purchase its policy. Before deciding to finance a policy through your insurance company, you should compare the interest rate to other borrowing rates and to other uses of these funds.

3. *One-year policy paid annually, semiannually, quarterly, or monthly.*

Based on our review of MBL's insurance policies, the following summary of insurance coverage on its owned property is prepared:

				Payments Due	
		Last Payment			Subsequent to
Property	Payment Terms	Date	Amount	19X1	19X1
Plant	3 yr. paid in advance	3/31/19X0	$6,600	$ —	$6,600
Warehouse	1 yr. paid monthly	3/31/19X0	7,200	7,200	—
Office	1 yr. paid annually	6/30/19X0	5,600	5,600	—
Machinery	1 yr. paid quarterly	9/30/19X0	3,100	3,100	—
				$15,900	$6,600

In posting to the forecasting worksheet, we must again keep in mind that for income statement and balance sheet purposes, expenses must be allocated to the proper accounting period. Therefore, if we are preparing an annual forecast, $2,200 (⅓ × $6,600) of the plant insurance must be charged to expense during 19X1. If we were forecasting a monthly income statement and/or balance sheet, the annual amounts would have to be further allocated by monthly charges to expense.

In attempting to forecast premium increases, conversations with insurance brokers are often helpful. Remember that they are in the business of selling and are apt to quote premium prices to best serve their own interests. If, for example, a three-year, paid in advance policy is up for renewal, the insurance broker is apt to quote large premium increases in order to sell the "price protection" aspect of the policy. Since insurance is usually not a significant expense, even a 10% to 20% increase in rates will not materially affect the cash flow forecast.

DEPRECIATION

Although depreciation is an accounting concept designed to allocate costs, it has no effect on cash flow. However, if we are to include an income statement and a balance sheet in our forecast, we must include depreciation. We can either obtain depreciation calculations from MBL's accounting department or calculate them ourselves from the fixed asset policies employed by the company. Assume MBL uses the straight-line method of depreciation and annual depreciation expense on existing assets is $30,-000. This amount can then be posted to the forecasting worksheet.

Costs Related to Existing Leased Property, Plant, and Equipment

Costs that fall into this category are usually the easiest to forecast since they represent fixed payments on scheduled payment dates. A word of caution is necessary. Although most lease agreements provide for servicing, repairs, insurance, etc., some do not. Before attempting to forecast lease payments, each lease should be reviewed and a listing of all required payments prepared. To the extent that the lease agreement requires the lessee to pay for repairs, insurance, and other expenses, schedules similar to those used for owned property should be prepared and included in the forecast. The following is a typical list of cash charges required in addition to lease payments:

- Repairs and maintenance.
- Insurance.
- Usage charges (e.g., fee per copy produced by a duplicating machine).
- Supplies (e.g., paper and ink used for duplicating machines).
- Escalator clauses. These will be discussed in detail under "Factors to Be Considered in Leasing Decision."

In addition to reviewing the actual lease agreement, examination of past invoices will often supply much of the needed forecast information.

A review of MBL's leasing agreements reveal that the only equipment being leased is a computer terminal for the company's time-sharing system. This time-sharing system is currently used to prepare MBL's general ledger, payroll, invoices, and inventory control. In addition to a fixed monthly lease payment of $100, the company is required to pay the following charges:

- $.066 per entry processed
- 1.103 per billing statement prepared
- 20.00 per 100,000 bits of storage

We have also learned that MBL processes 10,000 entries per year, is currently using 300,000 bits of storage, and has 200 customers. Although MBL intends to grow at a rate of 10% a year, it does not intend to seek new customers. This information can now be used to project MBL computer rental costs for 19X1 as follows:

MBL Mfg. Co.
Calculation of Computer Costs for 19X1

Description	Number of Transactions	Projected Increase	Cost per Transaction	Total
Monthly lease payments	12	—	$ 100	$1,200(12 × $100)
Entry processing	10,000	10%	.066	726(11,000 × $.066)
Billing statements	200 per mo.	—	.092	221(200 × $.092 × 12)
Storage (per 100,000)	3	10%	20.00	66(3.3 × $20.00)
				$2,213

This total can now be posted to the forecasting worksheet.

Costs Related to Expected Acquisitions of Property, Plant, and Equipment

Often the sole purpose of preparing a cash flow forecast is to determine the ability and feasibility of acquiring or leasing a new building or piece of equipment. The effect of such a decision will completely alter the cash flow forecast. For example, the acquisition of a new machine for MBL would have the following effects on its cash forecast:

- Increased utilization of cash for a down payment
- Increased debt payments for any portion of the purchase that is financed
- Increased repairs and maintenance

- Increased insurance
- Increased production and consequently increased purchases of inventory
- Increased sales and accounts receivable as a result of increased production

Therefore, once a firm decision is made to acquire new equipment, each section of the forecast should be adjusted accordingly. Since such an acquisition would only duplicate other sections of this text, we have assumed that MBL has not acquired any new equipment. However, keep in mind that if a firm commitment has not been made and the forecast is being used to assist in the decision-making process, the above variables should be considered. (See Chapter 9 for a discussion of forecast sensitivity and the impact of "what if" circumstances on the forecast.)

Even though we have assumed that MBL will not acquire any new property, plant, and equipment, the remainder of this chapter will be devoted to reviewing the criteria and considerations necessary to evaluate whether a particular fixed asset should be purchased or leased.

FACTORS TO BE CONSIDERED IN PURCHASE DECISION

Total Purchase Costs

As you know from purchasing your home, your car, and other personal property, the actual price paid is usually significantly higher than the price quoted by the sales agent. So, too, with corporate purchases of property, plant, and equipment. The following is a summary of some of the costs that must be added to the actual purchase price in order to make the purchase decision and to subsequently forecast the purchase.

Commissions. Although commissions are usually paid by the seller, often the purchaser is required to pay them. In addition, corporations often hire individuals on a commission basis to perform market and feasibility studies prior to any large acquisition. Discussions with the individual responsible for such acquisitions or with brokers will indicate industry practice and provide some information on the amount of commissions. It may also be useful to examine existing bids on the job in order to estimate the potential amount of commissions.

Installation. If installation is provided by the seller or manufacturer of the asset, that individual can usually provide cost estimates. If installation will be done by outside contractors, they are usually more than willing to supply estimates and bids. Remember that even if the installation is to be performed by in-house personnel, any incidental costs such as additional wiring, special space modifications or additions, etc., should be added to the purchase price.

Sales Tax. In some states, sales tax can account for as much as 5% to 10% of the total purchase price. A telephone call to the state and local taxing authorities will disclose what equipment, if any, is subject to the tax and the appropriate tax rate.

Delivery. If the purchaser is to pay for delivery costs you must determine how the asset will be delivered. Once the method of delivery is determined, estimates can then be obtained from several shippers.

Interest. If the purchase of the equipment is to be financed rather than paid for in cash, interest to be incurred is an ongoing cost associated with the acquisition. A detailed discussion of how to calculate and forecast interest expense will be presented in Chapter 6.

Tax Benefits

The purchaser of equipment, buildings, and other fixed assets receives certain tax benefits that are not available to the lessee of the same equipment. In order to evaluate the true cost of the acquisition, the following tax advantages must be taken into consideration.

Investment Tax Credit. Subject to certain limitations, The Economic Recovery Tax Act of 1981 provides for an investment tax credit as follows:

Property with a 3-year recovery period	6%
Property with a 5-, 10-, or 15-year recovery period	10%

Thus, the total purchase price of a piece of qualified equipment will economically be reduced by the amount of the investment tax credit. The following calculation illustrates the cash savings generated by the use of the investment tax credit on several pieces of equipment.

Equipment	Hypothetical Cost	Capital Cost Recovery Period (Years)	Investment Tax Credit Percent	Investment Tax Credit Amount
Auto, light trucks, R&D equipment	$ 8,000	3	6%	$ 480
Most equipment	50,000	5	10%	5,000
Public utility property with ADR* midpoint from 18 to 25 years, railroad tank cars	60,000	10	10%	6,000
Public utility property with ADR midpoint over 25 years	75,000	15	10%	7,500
				$18,980

*Asset Depreciation Range

Depreciation. Current tax law permits depreciation as a deduction from gross income in calculating taxable income. Therefore, assuming a corporation pays 46% in federal taxes, every $1 of depreciation saves the company $0.46 in federal taxes. Accelerated depreciation methods, which are allowable for tax purposes, will provide an even greater tax savings.

Interest. Current tax law also permits the interest portion of debt payments as a deduction in calculating taxable income. This, too, will reduce a company's tax expense.

Availability of Funds

Unless we intend to purchase the building or equipment for cash, we will need to finance at least a portion of the purchase price. Our "as is" cash flow will tell us how much cash will be available for the purchase. The difference, however, will have to be financed.

Most banks and other financers require an initial down payment before they will finance the remaining purchase price. Once we have determined that we can meet this initial requirement, we must still determine who will finance the remainder of the purchase and the rate to be charged. The best way to determine the lender and the borrowing rate is to ask the following potential sources of financing.

Banks. Those banks with which an ongoing business relationship exists are often most willing to finance acquisitions of this type. The reason for this is they probably know more about the financial history and cash flow of the company than anyone else. After all, they have continually evaluated the creditworthiness of the company in connection with prior and existing loans.

Real Estate Brokers. Typically, individuals selling large commercial real estate properties are familiar with the types and terms of financing available for similar acquisitions.

Mortgage Brokers. These brokers specialize in arranging financing for large commercial acquisitions. Since their commissions are based solely on their ability to locate and arrange for financing, they can identify lenders and provide interest rate estimates.

The Seller. Vendors of large equipment usually are more than willing to provide financing for their products and to discuss their terms in their sales presentations. Even sellers of real estate properties such as warehouses, plants, officers, etc. are often willing to finance the transactions themselves in order to make the sale. In general, however, sellers charge rates that are higher than outside financing rates and therefore should be considered the last resort.

Alternative Uses of Funds

As discussed throughout this text, it is assumed that you can do better by investing in your business than by investing in other things, including short-term funds, or you should not be in that business. However, a careful investigation of other uses of the funds—for example, repayment of existing debt or money market investments—is only prudent. Alternate use of funds should be carefully weighed against the long-term goals of the company.

Growth Potential

Unless a building or piece of equipment is being purchased to replace an existing building or piece of equipment, the new asset will normally increase production. At this juncture, a market study should be performed to ensure that such increased production can be sold at a profit. The marketplace must be able to absorb the new merchandise at a price that will cover the new costs plus provide an acceptable profit margin. Any purchase versus lease comparison presupposes that such a market study has proved a need for the new equipment.

FACTORS TO BE CONSIDERED IN LEASING DECISION

Up-Front Costs

In addition to installment and delivery costs which sometimes must be borne by the lessee, the lessee may also incur costs to modify existing space or other initial up-front costs. A careful reading of the proposed lease agreement will outline those costs that must be borne by the lessee.

Lease Payments

Under the lease agreement, the lessee is required to make periodic lease payments that reduce cash flow.

Escalator Clauses

Many lease arrangements, especially long-term leases, require periodic increases to the base lease rate as a hedge against rising expenses. Typically, these increases are pegged to outside inflation indicators. However, as a practical matter, there is a wide variety of methods used to calculate escalator clauses. Some of the more common methods used are as follows.

Fixed Percentage Increases at Predetermined Renewal Dates. This method is by far the easiest to calculate. By merely reading the lease agreement, we can determine the increased lease costs. For example, a 30-year warehouse lease might provide for a 15% increase every five years. Therefore, in preparing a cash flow forecast, we merely need to determine if any increases are due during the forecast period and, if so, to provide for the appropriate increase.

Increases Pegged to Inflation Indexes, for Example the Consumer Price Index (CPI). These increases are more difficult to project since they are dependent on an outside source. However, trends and forecasts of these indicators can be found in government reports and trade publications. As a practical matter, these indexes increase or decrease in direct proportion to inflation. For example, a lease on an office building might state that a 12% increase in the CPI may require a 12% increase in the base lease payment. Thus if our base lease payment is $50,000 and we project a 12-point increase in the Consumer Price Index, our lease payment would increase to $56,000 ($50,000 × 112%).

Increases Based on "Pass Through" Expenses Such as Tax, Utilities, etc. These increases are most often found in leases for shopping centers or office buildings. For example, the lease on office space may stipulate that in any year when taxes exceed $10,000, the amount of taxes due on the date the lease was signed, the lessee must pay the difference. Thus, if we are estimating annual property taxes of $13,000 for 19X1, an additional lease payment of $3,000 ($13,000 − $10,000) would be required.

Typically, escalator clause payments are made annually on the anniversary date of the lease. However, the lease should be read carefully to determine when and how such escalators are payable.

Tax Benefits

The monthly lease payments made by a lessee represent normal business expenses and as such represent a deduction in obtaining the lessee's taxable income. Therefore, for a lessee who is in a 46% tax bracket, each dollar of lease payments is only costing 54 cents because of the 46-cent tax benefit.

PURCHASE VERSUS LEASE COMPARISON

The ultimate decision to purchase or lease a specific piece of equipment or building should be based on which alternative presents the "best" economic deal. Since both the purchased and the leased asset are physically identical, the only difference is in the financing method. Because different companies have different tax structures and require different rates of return on their investments, it may be economically beneficial for one company to lease a machine or building while it may be more beneficial for another company to purchase it. In addition, the timing and amount of cash outflow differ with a purchase or lease transaction. As a result, we must find a method that will value the cash and convert both the purchase and lease transactions to a comparable basis.

Present Valuing

Compound financial tables can be used to provide a common denominator for evaluating the different streams of cash flow of both the purchase and the lease deal. For example, if the expected rate of return on investment for your company is 12%, then each outflow can be evaluated by *present valuing* the stream of cash at 12% and then deciding which is the cheapest financing method since both streams have been valued at the same point in time (i.e., today).

For illustrative purposes, let's assume that MBL is faced with the decision to either purchase or lease a new bending machine. We are told that MBL expects at least a 12% rate of return on all of its investments and that its effective tax rate is 40%. A bending machine has a four-year useful life, at the end of which time its scrap value is $6,000. The following cost information is available for each of the financing alternatives:

If Purchased:

Manufacturer's cost	$38,000
State and local tax	8%
Freight	1,200
Installation costs	1,600
Required down payment	20%
Monthly payments on amount financed	771
Interest rate	10%
Method of depreciation	Straight-line, 5-yr. property

If Leased:

Installation costs to be borne by lessee	$ 800
Monthly lease payments	1,000
Number of payments	48
Escalator payments—beginning in the third year, shall be equal to 2% for every 5-point increase in the Consumer Price Index in that year (MBL has projected that the Consumer Price Index for business machines will increase by 10 points per year over the next five years).	

We are now ready to calculate the value of each alternative. Table 5-6 shows the cost of purchasing the bending machine; Table 5-7 shows the cost of leasing it. Based on these analyses, it would be more economical to purchase the machine at at effective cost of $22,203 than to lease it at an effective cost of $24,583.

Often a corporation is required to choose between two purchase alternatives, such as buying a machine that produces 3,000 units per day as compared to one that produces 4,000 units per day. Although a present value analysis similar to the above analysis can be employed, there are two additional methods available, as the following discussion explains.

Table 5-6
MBL Mfg. Co.
Present Value Calculation Assuming Purchase of New Bending Machine

Cost			Present Value		
Description	Amount	Payment Dates	Table Used	Factor	Amount
Down payment	$7,600	Present	—	—	$ 7,600
Taxes ($38,000 × 8%)	3,040	Present	—	—	3,040
Freight	1,200	Present	—	—	1,200
Installation	1,600	Present	—	—	1,600
Investment tax credit* (10%)	4,384	Annually	Present worth of $1 at 12% annually	.8929	(3,914)
Debt service	771	Monthly	Present worth of $1 per period at 12% monthly	37.9739	29,278
Tax benefit of depreciation† ($43,840 ÷ 5 × 40%)	3,507	Annually	Present worth of $1 per period at 12% annually	3.0373	(10,652)
Tax benefit of interest deduction:‡					
Year 1	1,099	Annually	Present worth of $1 at 12% annually	.8929	(981)
Year 2	826	Annually	Present worth of $1 at 12% annually	.7972	(658)
Year 3	526	Annually	Present worth of $1 at 12% annually	.7118	(374)
Year 4	193	Annually		.6355	(123)
Scrap value	6,000	After 4 years	Present worth of $1 at 12% annually	.6355	(3,813)
			Total effective cost		$22,203

*Investment tax credit. Assumes that the machine will be purchased at the beginning of the tax year and therefore the company will have to wait one year until it files its tax return and obtains the tax benefit.

†Tax benefit of depreciation. Since tax returns are filed annually, the corporation must wait until the end of each year to obtain this tax benefit.

‡Tax benefit of interest deductions. Since only the interest portion of the $771 is deductible for tax purposes, we must calculate the annual interest paid each year before calculating the tax benefit. The annual interest amount can be obtained by manually calculating the principle and interest portion of the payments, or obtaining an amortization table, or reviewing a loan progress chart. See Chapter 3 for detailed discussion of each of these methods. The following calculations can then be made:

Year	Interest Amount	Tax Rate, %	Amount of Benefit
1	$2,747	40	$1,099
2	2,066	40	826
3	1,314	40	526
4	482	40	193

Table 5-7

MBL Mfg. Co.

Present Value Calculation Assuming Lease of New Bending Machine

Cost			Present Value		
Description	Amount	Payment Dates	Table Used	Factor	Amount
Installation	$ 800	Present	—	—	$ 800
Lease payments	1,000	Monthly	Present worth of $1 at 12% monthly	37.9739	37,974
Tax benefit of lease payment ($1,000 × 12 × 40%)	4,800	Annually	Present worth of $1 per period at 12% annually	3.0373	(14,579)
Escalator payments (net of tax):					
Year 3 ($12,000 × 4%)	480	Annually	Present worth of $1 at 12% annually	.7118	342
Year 4 ($12,000 × 4%)	480	Annually	Present worth of $1 at 12% annually	.6355	305
Tax benefits of escalator:					
Year 3 ($480 × 40%)	192	Annually	Present worth of $1 at 12% annually	.7118	(137)
Year 4 ($480 × 40%)	192	Annually	Present worth of $1 at 12% annually	.6355	(122)
			Total effective cost		$24,583

Payback Period

The payback period calculates the length of time it takes for each of the two alternative purchases to pay for itself (i.e., how long it takes to recover the initial investment cost). The payback period is determined as follows:

$$\frac{\text{Total net investment cost}}{\text{Annual net cash (after tax) flow}}$$

To illustrate, let's compare the purchase of two different machines, assuming the following:

	Machine 1	Machine 2
Manufacturer's cost	$38,000	$30,000
State and local tax	3,040	2,400
Freight	1,200	1,000
Installation cost	1,600	1,600
Depreciation method	straight-line, 5-yr. property	straight-line, 10-yr. property
Effective tax rate	40%	40%
Useful life	4 years	10 years
Gross annual earnings generated from increased production from machine	$18,000	$12,000

Table 5-8
MBL Mfg. Co.
Calculation of Payback Period for Machine 1 and Machine 2

	Machine 1	Machine 2
Costs:		
Manufacturer's cost	$38,000	$30,000
State and local taxes	3,040	2,400
Freight	1,200	1,000
Installation	1,600	1,600
Subtotal	$43,840	$35,000
Less: Investment tax credit		
($43,840 × 10%)	(4,384)	
($35,000 × 10%)		(3,500)
Total net costs	$39,456	$31,500
Tax expense:		
Annual Gross Income	$18,000	$12,000
Less: Depreciation		
($43,840 ÷ 5 yrs.)	(8,768)	
($35,000 ÷ 10 yrs.)		(3,500)
Taxable income	9,232	8,500
Tax rate	40%	40%
Tax expense	$ 3,693	$ 3,400
Annual net cash flow:		
Annual gross income	$18,000	$12,000
Tax payments	(3,693)	(3,400)
Total annual net cash flow	$14,307	$ 8,600
Payback Period		
Total net investment cost	$\frac{39,456}{14,307} = 2.76$	$\frac{31,500}{8,600} = 3.66$
Payback period	2.76 years	3.66 years

As you can see on Table 5-8, machine 1 has a shorter payback period than machine 2. However, although machine 1 will pay for itself in 2.76 years, it will only have 1.24 years of productive life left (4 − 2.76), while machine 2 will have 6.34 years of productive life left (10 − 3.66). The fact that the payback period method does not consider useful lives is its major shortcoming. Therefore, it cannot be considered an adequate indicator of risk. "When the payback method is used, it is more appropriately treated as a

[1]James Van Horne, *Financial Management and Policy*, 5th ed., Prentice-Hall, Englewood Cliffs, New Jersey, 1980, p. 113.

constraint to be satisfied than as a profitability measure to be maximized."[1] In addition this method is especially useful when comparing two alternatives with the same useful life.

Internal Rate of Return

The internal rate of return on an investment represents the present-value rate at which the stream of cash generated by the investment equals the investment cost. The investment alternative with the higher internal rate of return represents the more economical choice. Unlike the payback period, this method takes into consideration the useful lives of the alternatives. However, this method, too, has a shortcoming: The mathematical computations involved in this method are best suited to computer analysis. We can, however, mathematically approximate the internal rates of return by using a hit-and-miss approach. This approach merely takes the cash streams of each of the alternative investments and discounts them to various present value rates until a rate approximating the investment cost is found.

For illustrative purposes, let's calculate the internal rates of return for machine 1 and machine 2 in our previous example. The key information is summarized as follows:

	Machine 1	Machine 2
Net cost for investment	$39,456	$31,500
Annual net (after tax) cash flow	14,307	8,600
Expected cash flow period	4 years	10 years

Based on this information, internal rate of return for each machine is calculated in Table 5-9.

Since the net investment cost ($40,034 + $39,247 ÷ 2 = $39,640 vs. $39,456), is equal to an amount which falls between the present value of the annual net cash flow at 16% and the present value of the annual net case flow at 17%, the internal rate of return on machine 1 is just slightly over 16½%.

Since the present value of the annual net cash flow at 24% is almost equal to the net investment cost ($31,664 vs. $31,500), the internal rate of return on Machine 2 is 24%.

Note that in this analysis, machine 2 is a better economic buy than machine 1. This is because this method gives recognition to the fact that machine 2 has a longer productive life. Therefore, even though it will take longer to pay for itself (payback period of 3.66 years versus 2.76 years), it will be able to generate more cash flow.

Table 5-9
MBL Mfg. Co.
Internal Rate of Return for Machines 1 and 2

Discount Rate, %	Annual Net Cash Flow	Present Value	
		Factor	Amount
Machine 1 (Present worth of $14,307 annually for 4 years)			
14	$14,307	2.9137	$41,686
15	14,307	2.8550	40,846
16	14,307	2.7982	40,034
17	14,307	2.7432	39,247
Machine 2 (Present worth of $8,600 annually for 10 years)			
14	$ 8,600	5.2161	$44,858
15	8,600	5.0188	43,162
16	8,600	4.8332	41,566
17	8,600	4.6586	40,064
18	8,600	4.4941	38,649
19	8,600	4.3389	37,315
20	8,600	4.1925	36,056
21	8,600	4.0541	34,865
22	8,600	3.9232	33,740
23	8,600	3.7993	32,674
24	8,600	3.6819	31,664
25	8,600	3.5705	30,706

Exhibit 5-1

MBL Mfg. Co.

Forecasting Worksheet for the Year Ended 12/31/19X1

	Cash Flow			Income Statement			Balance Sheet				
	Repairs and Maintenance	Lease Payments	Other	Repairs and Maintenance	Other Expenses	Depreciation	Cash	PP&E Leaseholds	Accumulated Depreciation	Prepaid Insurance	Retained Earnings
Scheduled repairs:											
Service contracts	$(27,600)			$(27,600)			$ (27,600)				$ (27,600)
In-house	(3,745)			(3,745)			(3,745)				(3,745)
Unscheduled repairs	(10,000)			(10,000)			(10,000)				(10,000)
Property taxes			$(44,900)		$(44,900)		(44,900)				(44,900)
Insurance:											
Cash			(15,900)		(15,900)		(15,900)				(15,900)
Prepaid					(2,200)					$(2,200)	(2,200)
Depreciation						$(30,000)			$(30,000)		(30,000)
Lease payments		$(2,313)			(2,213)		(2,213)				(2,213)
	$(41,345)	$(2,213)	$(60,800)	$(41,345)	$(65,213)	$(30,000)	$(104,358)		$(30,000)	$(2,200)	$(136,558)

83

CHAPTER

Types of Debt

Basically, there are four types of debt: fixed rate debt, variable rate debt, fixed payment debt, and variable payment debt. These four types of debt are not mutually exclusive. For example, you can have fixed rate debt with a fixed or variable payment schedule. Let's now review each of these four categories and determine the factors that affect the timing and amount of principal and interest payments.

FIXED RATE DEBT

With this type of debt, the interest rate is assigned or fixed at the date the debt is incurred. Therefore, the only variable in forecasting this type of debt is the timing of its payment. Some examples of fixed rate debt are: corporate notes or bonds, mortgages, bank loans, and accounts payable.

VARIABLE RATE DEBT

In the past several years, inflation has continued to rise and interest rates have fluctuated as much as 5 points within a period of a few months. It is, therefore, no wonder that lenders are hesitant to make long-term fixed rate loans. As a result, lenders have attempted to create innovative methods of financing as a hedge against large interest-cost variations. The most innovative of these financing methods has been in the mortgage financing area. Some of the most common innovative methods are as follows.

1. *Variable rate.* Typically, the interest rate on this type of debt is indexed to the lending institutions' own cost of funds. For example, certain lending institutions will make loans, depending on the creditworthiness of their customers, at rates 1 to 5 points over their cost of funds rate.

2. *Renegotiable rate.* Under this type of arrangement, the lending institution permits a renegotiation of interest rates at specified intervals. For example, a loan may be made for a relatively short period of time, say six months, at which time it is understood that the lender will extend the loan but at the then-current market interest rate.

3. *Graduated rate.* Typically, the interest rate on this type of loan is fixed for the life of the loan. However, the loan agreement specifies stated interest increases at various intervals. For example, a loan may be made at an initial 13% interest rate with increases of, say, ½% each year over the life of the loan.

In order to forecast these types of debts, we must first review the loan agreements for provisions that call for rate increases. Then we must project the base on which such increases are dependent; for example, the prime rate. As we discussed in Chapter 3, there is no sure way of projecting future interest rates. In a short-term forecast, it may be beneficial to discuss rate trends with your bankers since they are responsible for setting the prime rate. However, the longer the forecast period, the more difficult projecting rates becomes. Because of this difficulty in projecting long-term interest rates and other long-range variables, Chapter 9 discusses forecast sensitivity and flexibility. In this chapter, we will learn how to quantify the effect of rate changes on the cash flow forecast.

FIXED PAYMENT DEBT

Like the fixed interest rate, the principal repayment terms of this type of debt are fixed at the date the debt is incurred. Here, too, the only forecasting variable is the timing of the contractual principal payments. Typically, corporate notes and bonds and bank loans have fixed payment terms.

VARIABLE PAYMENT DEBT

The most common variable payment debt is the *revolving credit* or *bank line of credit.* Under these two types of arrangements, banks will permit you to borrow, repay, and reborrow up to a predetermined limit at your option. The interest rate on this type of arrangement is usually variable.

However, these borrowing arrangements usually have a fixed term at which time all borrowings (drawdowns) must be repaid. Because both borrowings and repayments are made at the company's option, they can best be forecasted in connection with the sensitivity section of the forecast. Only after the entire forecast is complete can we determine the amount of cash, if any, that is available to repay these borrowings or the amount of new borrowing that is required.

Forecasting Debt

In preparing the forecast workpapers, it is often easiest if we divide debt into two broad categories, existing debt and projected debt.

EXISTING DEBT

The easiest approach to projecting interest and principal payments on existing debt is to first prepare a summary of terms on all existing debt. To illustrate, a summary of MBL's current outstanding debt is shown in Table 6-1.

TABLE 6-1
MBL Mfg. Co.
Summary of Current Outstanding Debt

			Payment Schedule	
Amount	Type	Interest Rates	Interest	Principal
$500,000	Senior debentures	8%	Jan. 1 and July 1	$500,000 July 19X3
$200,000	Subordinated debentures	12%	Mar. 31 and Sept. 30	$100,000 Sept. 19X1
				$100,000 Sept. 19X2
$500,000	Inventory financing	13%	Maturity	$500,000 Dec. 31, 19X5
$ 25,000	Graduated payment mortgage	11% until June 15, 19X1	Monthly	$ 1,000 end of each mo.
		12% until Dec. 15, 19X1		
		13% until June 15, 19X2		
$ 50,000	Renegotiable debt	12% until June 30, 19X1	Monthly	$ 50,000 Dec. 31, 19X3
$100,000	$600,000 revolving credit	Prime + 2%	Monthly	—

Now that we've summarized all of the outstanding debt, we can prepare detailed schedules computing the principal and interest payments due on each debt issue. Remember, for accounting purposes, interest expense must be accrued even though payment is deferred until the following period. Since we are preparing an income statement, in addition to our cash flow forecast, the schedules shown in Tables 6-2 and 6-3 have been prepared to facilitate forecasting timing differences between expense accruals and payments.

TABLE 6-2

MBL Mfg. Co.

Calculation of Principal and Interest Payments for 19X1 on Senior Debentures

	Payments		
Month	**Interest**	**Principal**	**Interest Accrual**
January ($500,000 × 8% × 1/2)	$ 20,000	$ —	$ 3,333($500,000 × 8% × 1/12)
February			3,333
March			3,334
April			3,333
May			3,333
June			3,334
July ($500,000 × 8% × 1/2)	20,000		3,333
August			3,333
September			3,334
October			3,333
November			3,333
December			3,334
Total	$ 40,000	$ —	$ 40,000

TABLE 6-3

MBL Mfg. Co.

Calculation of Principal and Interest Payments for 19X1 on Subordinated Debentures

	Payments		
Month	**Interest**	**Principal**	**Interest Accrual**
January	$ —	$ —	$ 2,000 ($200,000 × 12% × 1/12)
February			2,000
March ($200,000 × 12% × 1/2)	12,000		2,000
April			2,000
May			2,000
June			2,000
July			2,000
August			2,000
September ($200,000 × 12% × 1/2)	12,000	100,000	2,000
October			1,000 ($100,000 × 12% × 1/12)
November			1,000
December			1,000
	$ 24,000	$100,000	$21,000

The schedule shown in Table 6-2 would be required for a monthly forecast. However, since we are preparing an annual cash flow, the only calculation required would be as follows:

Principal amount	$ 500,000
Annual interest rate	8%
Annual interest	$ 40,000

This $40,000 interest payment can now be posted to the forecasting worksheet (Exhibit 6-1). Note that the principal of this debenture is due only at maturity in 19X3. Therefore, the current year's cash flow is affected only by interest payments.

Table 6-3 illustrates an important point on the timing of interest payments on debentures. Interest on debentures is usually paid every six months based on the outstanding balance of the previous six months. However, for accounting purposes, interest is calculated and accrued based on the balance outstanding during the month. For this reason, there is a $3,000 difference between interest expense ($21,000) and actual interest payments ($24,000). Both of these amounts, as well as the $100,000 principal payment, should be posted to the forecasting worksheet.

As indicated previously, our annual cash flow forecast would not require the above monthly calculations. Instead, only an annual calculation need be made. However, this calculation should reflect any changes in principal balances.

Before we forecast the inventory financing, we should note that the principal is not due until 19X4. In addition, we should note that interest, too, is not payable until maturity. Therefore, neither principal nor interest will have any effect on the current year's cash flow. For accounting purposes, however, interest must be accrued as follows:

Principal balance	$500,000
Annual interest rate	13%
Annual interest	$ 65,000

This $65,000 can now be posted to the Income Statement column of the forecasting worksheet.

In order to forecast the graduated payment mortgages, we merely plot out the monthly principal and interest payments according to the terms of the mortgage. This can be done as shown in Table 6-4.

TABLE 6-4

MBL Mfg. Co.

Monthly Principal and Interest Payment on Graduated Payment
Mortgage for the Year 19X1

Month	Principal Balance Beginning of Period	Interest Rate	Payment Principal	Payment Interest
January	$25,000	11%	$1,000	$ 229($25,000 × 11% ÷ 12)
February	24,000	11	1,000	220($24,000 × 11% ÷ 12)
March	23,000	11	1,000	211($23,000 × 11% ÷ 12)
April	22,000	11	1,000	202($22,000 × 11% ÷ 12)
May	21,000	11	1,000	193($21,000 × 11% ÷ 12)
June 1–15	20,000	11	—	92($20,000 × 11% ÷ 24)
June 16–30	20,000	12	1,000	100($20,000 × 12% ÷ 24)
July	19,000	12	1,000	190($19,000 × 12% ÷ 12)
August	18,000	12	1,000	180($18,000 × 12% ÷ 12)
September	17,000	12	1,000	170($17,000 × 12% ÷ 12)
October	16,000	12	1,000	160($16,000 × 12% ÷ 12)
November	15,000	12	1,000	150($15,000 × 12% ÷ 12)
December 1–15	14,000	12	—	70($14,000 × 12% ÷ 24)
December 16–31	14,000	13	1,000	76($14,000 × 13% ÷ 24)
			$12,000	$2,243

The principal and interest payments shown in Table 6-4 can now be posted to the forecasting worksheet. Since there are 12 equal principal monthly installments of $1,000 plus interest, we could reduce the calculations required for an annual cash forecast by using an average balance and an average interest rate calculated as follows:

Average balance:

Balance beginning of year	$ 25,000
Payments ($1,000 × 12)	(12,000)
Balance end of year	$ 13,000
Average balance ($25,000 + $13,000 ÷ 2)	$ 19,000

Average interest rate:

11% × 5½ mo. =	60.5
12% × 6 mo. =	72.0
13% × ½ mo. =	6.5
	139
To average	÷ 12
	11.58%

Calculation:

Average balance	$ 19,000
Average rate	11.58%
Interest	$ 2,200

Since the difference is only $43 ($2,243 — $ 2,200), either amount could be used.

The $50,000 renegotiable debt can best be forecasted in two steps: first, interest at 12% until June 30, 19X1, and second, interest at the expected renegotiated rate for the period June 30, 19X1 to December 31, 19X1. In order to project the estimated rate at which the loan will be renegotiated, we must first examine the lender's past practice concerning rate negotiations. In the past MBL has found that this particular lender has charged 3 points over the prime rate. Even if MBL did not have past renegotiation experience with this particular lender, a lender's current practices would provide a clue to future rates.

Now that we estimate a renegotiation rate of 3 points over prime, we still need to project what the prime rate will be at June 30, 19X1. As we discussed in Chapter 3, this can be done through talks with various lending institutions. Remember that this type of debt should be considered rate-sensitive debt and included in the sensitivity section of the forecast (see Chapter 9). Nevertheless, MBL is projecting a 16% prime rate on June 30, 19X1. Therefore, the calculations can be made as follows:

Principal	Annual Rate	Monthly Interest	No. of Months	Total
$50,000	12%	$500 ($50,000 × 12% ÷ 12)	6	$ 3,000
$50,000	16% + 3	$792 ($50,000 × 19% ÷ 12)	6	4,752
				$ 7,752

Since no principal payments are due in 19X1, we can post the interest to the forecasting worksheet.

PROJECTED DEBT

In addition to assessing future acquisitions, one of the major reasons for preparing a long-range cash flow forecast is to evaluate the debt requirements of the company. This is especially true for large companies that have large amounts of long-term debt with balloon payments due at maturity in the not too distant future. For example, MBL has $500,000, 8% debentures that are due in three years. It is this year's cash flow forecast that will outline the actions necessary to assure that the debt can be successfully paid off.

In developing a strategy for meeting large scheduled debt maturities, we must first determine if our projected cash flow is sufficient to meet our repayment requirements. Even if it is, we must further determine if there is a higher and better use for the cash. For example, excess cash may be earmarked for acquisitions or increased inventory purchases. If this is the case, it should not be projected as being available for the repayment of debt.

If operating cash flow is not sufficient to meet the debt requirement or if it is programmed for alternate uses, there are several remaining options that a company can consider. Basically, a company may sell its existing assets, refinance its existing debt, issue new debt, or issue equity capital. The remainder of this chapter will discuss in detail each of these four options.

METHODS OF MEETING REPAYMENT REQUIREMENTS

Sell Existing Assets

If a company is considering selling its assets to finance scheduled debt repayments, it must analyze the total effect of the sale. Not only will the sale decrease the asset but there may be also a reduction in cash flow due to lost revenues. The asset, revenue, and cash flow reduction must be reflected in the forecast.

Refinance Existing Debt

A company may refinance existing debt by exchanging it, or *rolling it over*. Here we attempt to exchange with existing holders old debt for new debt, usually at a higher interest rate. If the debt is publicly held, this exchange usually requires registration with the Securities and Exchange Commission. Since this registration process can take as long as six months to a year, it is advisable to make the exchange well in advance of the scheduled maturity date of the old debt. This allows time for the offer to take place and to permit alternate strategies if the offer is unsuccessful. Also, individuals are more likely to exchange lower-rate debt for new, higher-rate debt if they know they will have to hold their old low-rate debt a year or more to maturity.

With an exchange offer, three key elements must be forecasted:

1. The timing of the exchange
2. The new interest rate for the new debt
3. The amount of old debt that will be exchanged

If a public exchange offer is being contemplated, conversations with investment bankers will usually give you some idea as to the rate and timing of the offer. For private exchange offers, management can probably furnish rate and timing estimates that will be used in negotiations with would-be holders. Once the new interest rate is estimated, the differential between the old and new rates should be reflected in the cash flow forecast. This differential will be the only item in the exchange that affects cash flow, since the principal amount of the debt is merely being replaced with new debt, not being repurchased for cash. Remember that any debt that is not exchanged must be retired at maturity for cash.

The sensitivity section of a cash flow forecast is especially important here, since it will allow us to analyze the effect of different interest rates and exchange ratios. For example, we can determine the effect of exchanging 25% of existing debt for new debt at interest rates of 10%, 12%, 15%, or any other interest rate we project. We can further determine the effect of exchanging 50% or even 100% of our existing debt.

Issue New Debt

This financing strategy involves issuing new debt to new holders and then retiring the old debt for cash. As with an exchange offer, the rate, timing, and success ratio are the key elements to be projected. Again, these factors are best obtained by discussions with a company's investment bankers. However, unlike the exchange offer, a new issue will affect the cash flow, not only for the interest differential but also for principal receipts and disbursements. For example, cash from the new issue may be expected to be received several months prior to the repurchase of the old debt. The cash flow must therefore reflect interest on the old debt *and* interest on the new debt. In addition, the funds from the new debt offering must be employed from the new issue date to the redemption date of the old issue. Any earnings on this investment should also be included in the cash flow.

In forecasting an exchange offer or a new issue, one of the most important elements to include in the cash forecast is the cost of the exchange or issue. In a registration with the Securities and Exchange Commission, the following fees should be carefully estimated and included in the forecast:

Accounting fees
Legal fees
Printing costs
Underwriters' fees
Registration fees
"Blue sky" fees
Other fees

For a typical registration, these fees can run into hundreds of thousands of dollars. Since the amounts vary widely based on the circumstances of the offering, the individuals responsible for each function (i.e., auditors, lawyers, underwriters, etc.) should be contacted and asked to provide fee estimates.

Regardless of whether old debt is redeemed through operating cash flow or the proceeds from a new issue, the price at which old debt can be repurchased must be estimated. If we are anticipating short-term repurchases of debt, prices can usually be obtained from market quotations, if the debt is publicly held, or through conversations with lenders if the issue is privately held. Private investors and even banks will often accept payment, at a discount, of fixed rate debt in an environment of increasing interest rates.

If we are planning longer-range purchases, we must forecast future interest rates and then discount the obligation. For example, if MBL anticipates redeeming its 8% debentures two years prior to maturity (July 1, 19X2) at a time when interest rates are forecasted to be 13%, it could calculate its repurchase price by discounting the cash flow as follows:

Cash Stream	No. of Periods	Value Factor Based on 13%	Value
$500,000	4	.7773	$ 388,650
$ 20,000 ($500,000 × 8% × 1/2)	4	4.1557	83,114
			$ 471,764

Thus MBL could repurchase its 8% debentures in July of 19X2 for $471,764, an accounting gain of $28,236 ($500,000 − $471,764).

Issue Equity Capital

Although the financial implications are significantly different, mechanically there is little difference between forecasting a new debt issue and forecasting a new equity issue (i.e., common stock). The investment bankers can again assist us in projecting the timing and amount of cash. However, there is one significant difference: After receipt of the proceeds, there is no ongoing interest expense that must be forecasted.

Factoring Receivables

In reviewing methods of obtaining financing, we should consider the effects of secured financing, or *factoring*. Mention of the term factoring tends to conjure up images of the small manufacturing company selling its soul to the devil. In reality, the factoring of receivables is done by large, successful companies. Also, it is often done by companies far removed from the manufacturing industry. For example, banks and mortgage companies often sell *participations* in their mortgages. Drilling and mining companies often sell participations in their drilling or mining operations.

The terms of factoring agreements vary from company to company and industry to industry. However, these deals typically work as follows. The company will "sell" its receivable (accounts receivable, mortgage receivable, etc.) to a third party at a discount. As the receivable is collected, it is remitted to the "purchaser." Often, the "seller" will guarantee the receivable, and must repay the "purchaser" for any defaulted accounts.

This type of transaction, "selling" a non-interest-bearing receivable at a discount, is in essence a means of obtaining a loan that is repaid through the cash collected on the receivable. The discount is, in reality, the interest paid to the lender.

In forecasting this type of transaction, we must estimate both of the following:

1. The receipt of the expected selling price
2. The payout of the collections on the receivables

For illustrative purposes, let's assume that MBL will sell its December 19X1 accounts receivable in order to raise funds. Let's further assume that the loan rates for factored receivables in December are expected to be 18%. Assuming a 60-day collection period on the receivable, we must first calculate a selling price. This can be done by discounting the amount to be collected for two monthly periods (60 days) as follows:

Balance of December receivable	$ 268,070
Present worth of 1 factor at 18% for	
two periods	.9707
	$ 260,215

We are now ready to post the effect of the above on our cash flow forecast. Depending on the circumstances, the loss of $7,855 ($268,070 − $260,215) will, for accounting purposes, be either charged to expense in December or deferred and written off as interest expense in January and February. For our purposes, let's defer the loss. In posting to the forecasting worksheet, we can show receipt of cash in 19X1 of $260,215 and a reduction of accounts receivable by $268,070. However, we must be especially careful not to project any cash receipts for the December sales in the following period. One easy way to prevent this is to record the $268,070 reduction of accounts receivable in 19X1 as a contra asset or liability. In this way, any subsequent cash receipts would be earmarked for payment to the "factors."

Short versus Long-Term Debt

Any discussion of debt financing must address the question of long- versus short-term debt. This text deals with the methods of forecasting cash flow, not with managing a company's financing. It is presumed that the decision on the type of financing that best suits your company has already been made. However, there are certain characteristics of long- and short-term debt that may prove helpful in the forecasting process.

1. *Matching assets and liabilities.* Typically, financial managers try to finance short-term assets with short-term liabilities and corresponding long-term assets with long-term debt. By matching the two, you have "locked in" your financing expense. For example, if you need cash to pay for inventory purchases, it doesn't make sense to issue long-term debentures since the inventory will turn over into sales in a short period of time and will generate cash to repay any financing.

An extreme example of the dangers of mismatched funding was demonstrated by the REITs of the 1960s and 1970s. Some REITs made long-term mortgage loans with funds they obtained from drawing down their revolving bank lines. As a result, they had a fixed income stream (interest on long-term mortgage loans) and a variable expense stream (interest on short-term borrowings). As rates increased, the bank debt became more and more expensive without the benefit of increased income. As a result, many REITs went bankrupt.

2. *Rate differential.* As a general rule, long-term financing is cheaper than short-term financing. Usually, lenders assume that in the long term, periodic rises and dips in rates will level out, they will have less risk, and consequently they will accept a lower constant yield. At this writing, *The Wall Street Journal* indicated that the majority of corporate bonds were yielding 13% or less at a time when the prime rate was 16%.

3. *Pledging of assets.* Long-term debt is more likely to require collateral than short-term debt. For example, mortgages are usually secured by real estate. This may or may not hinder operating flexibility. If assets are pledged to secure debt, there are often restrictions placed on the sale of those assets.

Exhibit 6-1
MBL Mfg. Co.
Forecasting Worksheet for the Year Ended 12/31/19X1

| | Cash Flow | | | Income Statement | | | Balance Sheet | | | | | |
	Interest Payments	Principal Payments	Proceeds From Factoring	Interest Expense	Cash	Mortgages Payable	Deferred Interest Exp.	Interest Payable	Debentures	Factoring Liability	Retained Earnings
Senior debentures	$(40,000)			$ (40,000)	$ (40,000)						$ (40,000)
Subordinated debentures	(24,000)	$(100,000)		(21,000)	(124,000)			$ 21,000 (24,000)	$(100,000)		(21,000)
Inventory financing				(65,000)				65,000			(65,000)
Graduated payment Mtg.	(2,243)	(12,000)		(2,243)	(14,243)	$(12,000)					(2,243)
Renegotiable debt	(7,752)			(7,752)	(7,752)		$7,855				(7,752)
A/C rec. financing			$260,215		260,215					$268,070	
	$(73,995)	$(112,000)	$260,215	$(135,995)	$ 74,220	$(12,000)	$7,855	$ 62,000	$(100,000)	$268,070	$(135,995)

96

Other Areas to Be Forecasted

Each of the previous chapters has dealt with a specific area of the cash flow forecast. This chapter discusses a variety of miscellaneous items that must be considered and quantified for the forecast.

Salaries and Wages

For accounting purposes, salaries are either charged directly to expense or charged to cost of goods sold. Therefore, if an income statement and a balance sheet are to accompany the cash flow forecast, our forecasting workpapers should be set up to facilitate this division. Remember, in Chapter 4, "Inventories," we charged $10.00 per unit to cost of goods sold as a part of our standard costing. We must now calculate the amount of actual labor that must be included in our inventory balance.

In order to begin the forecasting process, we should break down salaries into various payment categories, that is, weekly, biweekly, monthly, semimonthly, etc. This is especially important in preparing monthly forecasts since some months have four payroll weeks while others have five. One of the easiest methods to accomplish this is to obtain a calendar for the forecast period, mark off the various paydays, and indicate the payment category each payday applies to. We have learned from Marge Everett, MBL's controller, that all employees below the level of vice president are paid weekly on Friday. All employees at the vice president level or above are paid monthly. We can now mark up a 19X1 calendar, using "O" to indicate weekly paydays and "X" to indicate monthly paydays.

```
          JANUARY                      FEBRUARY                      MARCH
  S  M  T  W  T  F  S          S  M  T  W  T  F  S          S  M  T  W  T  F  S
  1  2  3  4  5 (6) 7                   1  2 (3) 4                      1  2 (3) 4
  8  9 10 11 12(13)14          5  6  7  8  9(10)11          5  6  7  8  9(10)11
 15 16 17 18 19 20 21         12 13 14 15 16(17)18         12 13 14 15 16(17)18
 22 23 24 25 26 27 28         19 20 21 22 23(24)25         19 20 21 22 23(24)25
 29 30 X                      26 27 X                      26 27 28 29 30 X

           APRIL                         MAY                          JUNE
  S  M  T  W  T  F  S          S  M  T  W  T  F  S          S  M  T  W  T  F  S
                    1          1  2  3  4 (5) 6                         1 (2) 3
  2  3  4  5  6 (7) 8          7  8  9 10 11(12)13          4  5  6  7  8  9 10
  9 10 11 12 13(14)15         14 15 16 17 18(19)20         11 12 13 14 15(16)17
 16 17 18 19 20(21)22         21 22 23 24 25(26)27         18 19 20 21 22(23)24
 23 24 25 26 27(28)29         28 29 30 X                   25 26 27 28 29 X
 30

           JULY                        AUGUST                      SEPTEMBER
  S  M  T  W  T  F  S          S  M  T  W  T  F  S          S  M  T  W  T  F  S
                    1                   1  2  3 (4) 5                      1 (1) 2
  2  3  4  5  6 (7) 8          6  7  8  9 10(11)12          3  4  5  6  7 (8) 9
  9 10 11 12 13(14)15         13 14 15 16 17(18)19         10 11 12 13 14(15)16
 16 17 18 19 20(21)22         20 21 22 23 24(25)26         17 18 19 20 21(22)23
 23 24 25 26 27(28)29         27 28 29 30 X                24 25 26 27 28 X 30
 30 X

          OCTOBER                      NOVEMBER                      DECEMBER
  S  M  T  W  T  F  S          S  M  T  W  T  F  S          S  M  T  W  T  F  S
  1  2  3  4  5 (6) 7                   1  2 (3) 4                      1 (1) 2
  8  9 10 11 12(13)14          5  6  7  8  9(10)11          3  4  5  6  7 (8) 9
 15 16 17 18 19 20 21         12 13 14 15 16(17)18         10 11 12 13 14(15)16
 22 23 24 25 26(27)28         19 20 21 22 23(24)25         17 18 19 20 21(22)23
 29 30 X                      26 27 28 29 X                24 25 26 27 28(29)30
                                                           31
```

Now that we know the timing of salary payments, we should begin quantifying salaries. In order to do that, several factors must first be considered, as explained in the following discussion.

CURRENT BASE SALARY

This information can usually be obtained by examining payroll records. Elliot Green, director of personnel, has given you the following payroll summary of salaries for MBL employees:

4 bending machine operators	$210 per week
3 drill press operators	$230 per week
18 assemblers	$160 per week
3 clerical	$135 per week
2 salesmen	3% of gross sales

5 vice presidents	$35M per year
1 executive vice president	$55M per year
1 president	$75M per year

PROJECTED SALARY INCREASES

There are several different types of salary increases.

Annual Increases

Most companies give annual or semiannual raises to employees. Since both the timing and amount of these increases are under the direct control of management, these amounts can easily be projected. However, care should be exercised and estimated increases should be compared to government wage and price guidelines, especially for those industries that have government contracts.

Union Contracts

Most union contracts have cost-of-living and other salary increase provisions. Therefore, a review of these contracts will provide estimates of these increases.

Executive Contracts

Many key employees sign compensation contracts when they are hired. Like union contracts, these should be reviewed and any increases quantified for the forecast.

Elliot Green has indicated that although MBL has traditionally given 10% across-the-board salary increases, this year only a 7% raise will be given in order to comply with government guidelines. This is necessary due to MBL's new government contract. Mr. Green felt that this will be especially hard to explain to accounting and clerical personnel since they do not have union contracts. Since the union contract provided for only a 5% mandatory increase, MBL is expected to give a 6% increase to union workers and an 8% increase to nonunion workers, including officers, effective September 1.

Currently, only the president has an executive contract. His contract provides for a salary of $75,000, to be increased to $100,000 effective March 31, 19X1.

OVERTIME

Many companies pay overtime to employees working more than a specified number of hours. Overtime salary can be calculated once we know the base time period over which overtime is paid and the overtime rate (i.e., time and a half, double time, etc.). It is also helpful to review a company's past overtime history. A word of caution is in order. Management almost always projects the elimination of overtime. However, if overtime is a significant component of past salary expense, unless some positive action has been taken (i.e., more employees, less work, etc.) it is unlikely that overtime will disappear. MBL normally pays time and a half to all employees under the level of vice president. However, the only individuals authorized to work overtime are factory workers. Usually their overtime runs about 10% in the peak months of May through August.

COMMISSIONS

Employees on commission are paid on either a straight commission basis or a salary plus commission basis. It is important to review commission agreements in order to quantify the amounts involved. Both of MBL's salesmen are paid 3% of the current month's gross sales.

BONUSES

Many companies offer various bonus and/or incentive plans. Since these are determined by management, they are easy to forecast. The officers of MBL have been promised a bonus based on the following percentages of income before taxes in excess of $250,000.

Vice presidents	5%
Executive vice president	8%
President	10%

Bonuses are paid in February and are based on the previous December's year-to-date earnings.

INCREASED NUMBER OF EMPLOYEES

If additional employees are to be hired during the forecast period, the increased salary cost should also be included in the forecast. Discussions with management will usually provide this information. Elliot Green has informed you that MBL intends to hire an additional accounting clerk at $250 per week starting June 30, 19X1.

With all of the information we have on timing and amounts of compensation, we can now begin to forecast salary expense. One way of projecting cash flows is to prepare an annual forecast sheet for each employee or group of employees. This method is especially useful for companies with only a few employees or companies with computerized payroll systems. For illustrative purposes, we will prepare individual salary forecasts for only the assemblers, the salesmen, and the president, by month.

First, let's forecast salaries for the assemblers, as shown in Table 7-1.

Table 7-1

MBL Mfg. Co.

Assemblers' Salary Forecast for 19X1

Month	Weekly Base Pay	No. of Weeks	Base Pay	Overtime %	Overtime Amount	Total
Jan.	$2,880 (1)	4	$11,520	—	$ —	$ 11,520
Feb.	2,880	4	11,520	—	—	11,520
Mar.	2,880	5	14,400	—	—	14,400
Apr.	2,880	4	11,520	—	—	11,520
May	2,880	4	11,520	10	1,728 (3)	13,248
June	2,880	5	14,400	10	2,160	16,560
July	2,880	4	11,520	10	1,728	13,248
Aug.	2,880	4	11,520	10	1,728	13,248
Sept.	3,053 (2)	5	15,265	—	—	15,265
Oct.	3,053	4	12,212	—	—	12,212
Nov.	3,053	4	12,212	—	—	12,212
Dec.	3,053	5	15,265	—	—	15,265
Total Assemblers						$160,218
Machine Operators (4)						46,730
Drill Assemblers (4)						38,389
Total Factory						$245,337

(1) $160 × 18 = 2,880
(2) $160 × 18 = 2,880 + 6% = 3,053 (reflects 6% salary increase)
(3) $11,520 × 10% × 1.5 = 1,728 (reflects 10% overtime at time and a half)
(4) Calculations not shown. However, salary would be calculated in the same manner as assemblers' salary.

With an annual forecast, we can short-cut the calculations shown in Table 7-1 by using averages. For example, assemblers' salary could be calculated as follows:

Base salary for 8 months (30 weeks × $160 × 18)	$ 86,400
Base salary for 4 months after 6% salary increase (22 weeks × $160 × 18 × 106%)	67,162
Overtime for 4 months (17 weeks × $160 × 18 × 10% × 1.5)	7,344
Per averaging	$160,906
Per detailed calculations	$160,218

Since the difference is only $688 ($160,906 − $160,218), either method can be used.

Next, let's look at the salesmen. Since MBL's two salesmen are paid solely on a commission basis (3% of sales), we can calculate their salaries by simply taking 3% of monthly forecasted sales. In order to do this, we must first determine the amount of sales subject to commission. Items like recurring orders may not require commissions. We have learned that 90% of MBL's nongovernment sales are subject to commission. Therefore, we

Table 7-2
MBL Mfg. Co.
Salesman's Commission Forecast for 19X1

Month	Base Sales	Commission Rate	Commission Amount
Jan.	$181,800 (202,000 × 90%)	3%	$ 5,454
Feb.	183,600 (204,000 × 90%)		5,508
Mar.	185,490 (206,100 × 90%)		5,565
Apr.	206,118 (229.020 × 90%)		6,183
May	212,256 (235,840 × 90%)		6,368
June	218,592 (242,880 × 90%)		6,558
July	225,126 (250,140 × 90%)		6,754
Aug.	231,534 (257,260 × 90%)		6,946
Sept.	234,135 (260,150 × 90%)		7,024
Oct.	236,511 (262,790 × 90%)		7,095
Nov.	238,887 (265,430 × 90%)		7,167
Dec.	241,263 (268,070 × 90%)		7,238
			$77,860

can calculate commissions as shown in Table 7-2. Again, since we are pre-paring an annual cash flow, the calculations shown in Table 7-2 can be shortened as follows:

Total sales for 19X1	2,884,040
% of sales subject to commission	90%
Sales subject to commission	2,595,636
Commission rate	3%
Per averaging	$ 77,869
Per detailed calculations	$ 77,860

Again, since the difference is only $9 ($77,869 − $77,860), either method can be used. In general, however, the averaging method produces a close enough approximation to the detailed calculations that the detailed cal-culations are unnecessary.

Now let's forecast the president's salary, as shown in Table 7-3.

Table 7-3

MBL Mfg. Co.

President's Salary Forecast for 19X1

Month	Monthly Salary	Bonus	Total
January	$6,250 (1)	$ —	$ 6,250
February	6,250	11,200 (4)	17,450
March	6,250	—	6,250
April	8,333 (2)	—	8,333
May	8,333	—	8,333
June	8,333	—	8,333
July	8,333	—	8,333
August	8,333	—	8,333
September	9,000 (3)	—	9,000
October	9,000	—	9,000
November	9,000	—	9,000
December	9,000	—	9,000
			$107,615

(1) $75,000 ÷ 12 = 6,250
(2) $100,000 ÷ 12 = 8,333 (reflects increase due under executive contract)
(3) $8,333 + 8% = 9,000 (reflects 8% salary increase)
(4) $362,000   Earnings per 19X0 income statement
    (250,000)   Base on which no bonuses are paid
    112,000   Bonus base
    10%   President's bonus rate
    11,200   President's bonus

Again, the calculation shown in Table 7-3 can be shortened as follows:

Base salary for 3 months ($75,000 ÷ 12 × 3)	$ 18,750
Base salary for 5 months ($100,000 ÷ 12 × 5)	41,666
Base salary for 4 months ($100,000 + 8% ÷ 12 × 4)	36,000
Bonus (see previous calculation)	11,200
	$107,616

Bonuses for one fiscal year are usually paid early in the next fiscal year and are therefore relatively easy to calculate. However, if we are calculating bonuses for two forecast years, we must be sure to use earnings that we forecasted for the earlier forecast year. For example, if we wanted to calculate the president's bonus for the forecast year 19X2, it would be done as follows:

$	Earnings per 19X1 forecast
(250,000)	Base on which no bonuses are paid
	Bonus base
10%	President's bonus rate
$	President's bonus

The same techniques used to forecast both the assemblers' and the president's salaries can be used for the rest of MBL's employees. However, for illustrative purposes, let's assume that we have calculated all of the other employees' salaries, as follows:

Vice presidents	$207,620
Executive vice president	65,412
President	107,615
Clerical	21,615
New employees	6,500

Since we have all of the forecasted salary numbers, we can now post to the forecasting worksheet (Exhibit 7-1).

Federal Withholdings

There are three questions that must be answered in order to forecast the effect of withholding federal taxes on cash flow:

1. How much is going to be withheld?
2. When is it going to be withheld?
3. When is it going to be remitted to the federal government?

Federal taxes are withheld from an individual's salary check based on his or her filing status and the number of dependents claimed. However, unless an individual changes his or her status or exemptions, or the tax rates change, the withholdings will remain the same. Therefore, the easiest way to forecast withholdings is to first determine the percent of current salaries that is being withheld and then apply this same percentage to forecasted salaries.

Our review of MBL's payroll register reveals that current federal withholdings are running approximately 28% of gross salaries. It's important to note that variations from any "normal" withholding rate should be examined and accounted for. For example, many companies withhold a flat percentage for items like bonuses instead of calculating the appropriate withholdings using the normal withholding tables. Let's assume that withholdings on the MBL bonuses paid in February approximate 20%.

A key factor in forecasting federal withholding taxes is the timing of their payment to the government. Although taxes are withheld from each salary check, they are usually remitted to the federal government only on a quarterly basis. Therefore, the schedule presented in Table 7-4 can be used to calculate federal withholdings and remittances. We are now ready to post to the forecasting worksheet (Exhibit 7-1). Since we are preparing an annual forecast, there is no effect on cash flow because the amount withheld is equal to the amount remitted. However, a monthly cash flow for the first quarter might look something like the worksheet presented in Table 7-5.

Table 7-4

MBL Mfg. Co.

Federal Withholding Calculation for 19X1

Month	Monthly Salary*	Withholding Percentage	Bonus	Withholding Percentage	Amount† Withheld	Amount† Remitted
Jan.	$49,837	28%	$ —	—	$ 13,954	$ —
Feb.	49,837	28		—	13,954	—
			48,160	20%	9,632	
Mar.	55,988	28	—	—	15,677	53,217
Apr.	53,469	28	—	—	14,971	—
May	56,478	28	—	—	15,813	—
June	61,736	28	—	—	17,286	48,070
July	57,864	28	—	—	16,202	—
Aug.	58,056	28	—	—	16,256	—
Sept.	59,887	28	—	—	16,768	49,226
Oct.	55,277	28	—	—	15,478	—
Nov.	55,359	28	—	—	15,501	—
Dec.	70,011	28	—	—	19,603	50,582
					$201,095	$201,095

*Monthly salary was calculated by adding all of the individual salary calculations.
†Assumes that quarterly remittance is made within the quarter. If actual remittance for the quarter ended March 31 is made in April, the postings should be adjusted accordingly.

Table 7-5

MBL Mfg. Co.

Monthly Forecasting Worksheet for 19X1

	Cash Flow		Income Statement	Balance Sheet			
	Salaries	FIT Payments	Salary Expense	Cash	Inventory	FIT Payable	Retained Earnings
January							
	($49,837)	$	$ 26,758	($49,837)	$23,079	$	($26,758)
	13,954			13,954		13,954	
	(35,883)		26,758	(35,883)	23,079	13,954	(26,758)
February							
	(49,837)		26,758	(49,837)	23,079		(26,758)
	13,954			13,954		13,954	
	(48,160)		48,160	(48,160)			(48,160)
	9,632			9,632		9,632	
	(74,411)		74,918	(74,411)	23,079	23,586	(74,918)
March							
	(55,988)		28,391	(55,988)	27,597		(28,391)
	15,677			15,677		15,677	
		(50,308)		(50,308)		(50,308)	
	(40,311)	(50,308)	28,391	(90,619)	27,597	(34,631)	(28,391)
	(150,605)	$(50,308)	$130,067	$(200,913)	$73,755	$ 2,909	$(130,067)

The analysis of withholding taxes shown in Table 7-5 is also equally applicable for state, city, local tax, disability, and other withholding requirements.

FICA (Social Security) Withholdings

Forecasting FICA withholdings differs from forecasting federal tax withholdings for two reasons. First, there is a limit on the salary base to which FICA applies. Second, in addition to the portion withheld from the employee, the corporation must also pay a like amount.

As of this writing, the current summary of future FICA bases and rates as provided for under the Federal Insurance Contributions Act was as follows·

Year	Salary Base	FICA Rate, %
1979	$ 22,900	6.13
1980	25,900	6.13
1981	29,700	6.65
1982	30,000	6.70
1983	31,800	6.70
1984	33,600	6.70

The easiest way to forecast FICA withholdings is to group employees according to salary. For illustrative purposes, let's prepare the FICA forecast worksheets for the president, bending machine operators, and drill press operators. We can group drill press operators and bending machine operators together since their weekly salaries differ by only $20 ($230 vs. $210). A $20 difference for 7 operators, for 52 weeks at 6.13%, will result in a variance of only $446 ($20 × 7 × 52 × 6.13%), a difference that is clearly immaterial. As a practical matter, in preparing a forecast, it is usually a good idea to consider grouping together all individuals earning less than the FICA base. However, this should be determined on a case-by-case basis, depending on the degree of accuracy required and the variances in salary levels below the base. For example, if half of the employees below the FICA base earn $10,000 and the other half earn $20,000, this is probably a good grouping. For illustrative purposes let's prepare the schedule shown in Table 7-6. We've assumed the FICA base is $25,900 and the rate is 6.13%.

Table 7-6

MBL Mfg. Co.

19X1 FICA Forecast Worksheet for Bending and Drill Press Operators

Month	Total Salary	FICA Rate	Employee Portion	Employer Portion	Remitted
Jan.	$ 6,105	6.13%	$ 374	$ 374	$ —
Feb.	6,105	6.13	374	374	—
Mar.	7,632	6.13	468	468	2,432
Apr.	6,105	6.13	374	374	—
May	7,021	6.13	430	430	—
June	8,777	6.13	538	538	2,684
July	7,021	6.13	430	430	—
Aug.	7,021	6.13	430	430	—
Sept.	8,089	6.13	496	496	2,712
Oct.	6,472	6.13	397	397	—
Nov.	6,472	6.13	397	397	—
Dec.	8,299	6.13	509	509	2,606
	$85,119		$5,217	$5,217	$10,434

The monthly breakdown shown in Table 7-6 would again be required only if monthly forecasts must be prepared. For purposes of our annual forecast, the FICA withholdings could be simply calculated as follows:

Annual salary	$85,119
FICA rate	6.13%
	$ 5,217

Let's now move on to the president's FICA forecast, shown in Table 7-7. Remember, the employer portion of FICA for factory workers must be charged to inventory since it is a part of cost of goods manufactured. The employer portion of nonfactory workers must be charged to salary expense.

Table 7-7

MBL Mfg. Co.

19X1 FICA Forecast Worksheet for President

Month	Total Salary	FICA Rate	Amount		Remitted
			Employee Portion	Employer Portion	
Jan.	$ 6,250	6.13%	$ 383	$ 383	
Feb.	17,450(1)	6.13	1,070	1,070	
Mar.	6,250	6.13	135(2)	135	$3,176
Apr.	8,333				
May	8,333				

Table 7-7   (Cont.)

Month	Total Salary	FICA Rate	Amount Employee Portion	Amount Employer Portion	Remitted
June	8,333				
July	8,333				
Aug.	8,333				
Sept.	9,000				
Oct.	9,000				
Nov.	9,000				
Dec.	9,000				
	$107,615		$1,588	$1,588	$3,176

(1) Includes $11,200 bonus which is subject to FICA.
(2) Represents 6.13% of $2,200 because president has hit the FICA base limit:

January	$ 6,250
February	17,450
March	2,200
	$25,900

We can now summarize our calculations for MBL (see Table 7-8) and post them to the forecasting worksheet (Exhibit 7-1).

Table 7-8
MBL Mfg. Co.
Total 19X1 FICA Remittances

	Employee Portion	Employer Portion	Total Remitted
Factory workers:			
Bending and drill press operators	$ 5,217	$ 5,217	
Assemblers	9,821	9,821	
	$15,038	$15,038	$30,076
Nonfactory workers:			
Clerical	1,325	1,325	
Salesmen	3,175	3,175	
Vice presidents	7,938	7,938	
Executive vice president	1,588	1,588	
President	1,588	1,588	
New employee	398	398	
	$16,012	$16,012	$32,024
	$31,050	$31,050	$62,100

In connection with forecasting salaries, another significant area is pension benefits. In order to determine the effect of pension benefits on cash flow, we must first determine when these benefits are to be funded. Most companies fund their pension plan on an annual or semiannual basis. This can best be determined by reviewing the pension plan itself and the company's past policy.

Quantification of the amount of pension benefits to be funded must be based on the terms of the pension plan. If pension funding is based on actuarially computed amounts, then actuarial pro forma calculations should be made. On the other hand, if pension benefits are determined as a percentage of salaries or profits, then calculations should be based on forecasted salaries or profits. For example, if MBL's pension benefits are 10% of salary expense, then pension benefits for MBL could be calculated as follows:

	19X1	19X2	19X3
Forecasted salaries	$840,902	$1,029,267	$1,205,149
	10%	10%	10%
Forecasted pension benefits	$ 84,090	$ 102,927	$ 120,515

Accounting Fees

Accounting services can usually be broken down into three major categories:

1. Annual audit fees
2. Annual tax fees
3. Fees incurred for special projects

The best way to estimate these fees is to review prior years' expenditures and to obtain current estimates from the accountants. Fees for special projects must be based on the company's future expectations. For example, if the company anticipates acquiring a new subsidiary, the accountants may be engaged to perform a purchase investigation. Accounting services may also be required if the company anticipates putting in a new accounting system. If this is the case, we must then estimate:

• When the work will take place
• What the work will cost
• When the work must be paid
• How much of the cost can be deferred

Marge Everett, controller, has informed you that the audit fee for the current year is estimated to be $26,000 and that she will pay the bill in two installments—$13,000 when the annual report is completed in February 19X1 and $13,000 in April 19X1. She has also indicated that the annual fee for tax return preparation is $6,000 and that this bill will be paid in June 19X1. In addition, the auditors have informed her that the 19X1 audit will probably run about $30,000 as a result of billing rate increases.

Based on the above information, we can prepare the schedule of accounting fees shown in Table 7-9. Remember, the accruals for accounting services will be based on the estimated cost of the 19X1 audit while the payments made in 19X1 will relate to the 19X0 audit. We can now post the above amounts to the forecasting worksheet (Exhibit 7-1).

Table 7-9

MBL Mfg. Co.

Accounting Services Forecasting Worksheet for 19X1

		Amount	
Month	Service	Paid	Accrued
January	(1/12 estimated 19X0 fee: $30,0000 + 6,000)	$ —	$ 3,000
February	(1/2 19X0 audit fee: $26,000)	13,000	3,000
March		—	3,000
April	(1/2 19X0 audit fee: $26,000)	13,000	3,000
May		—	3,000
June	(Estimated tax fee)	6,000	3,000
July		—	3,000
August		—	3,000
September		—	3,000
October		—	3,000
November		—	3,000
December		—	3,000
		$32,000	$36,000

Utilities

Utilities such as water, light, power, etc., should be categorized for forecasting purposes as either *factory* utilities or *other* utilities. Factory utilities should be charged to inventory as part of the cost of goods manufactured. All other utilities should be charged to expense.

When forecasting utility costs, keep in mind that these costs can increase if the usage rises or if rates increase. In order to project increased usage, we must examine the utility bills to determine what portion is directly related to operations. For example, if factory machinery runs on electricity and we have previously projected a 3% productivity increase, then the portion of electricity that relates to that machinery will increase proportionately. Moreover, if we have projected the purchase of an additional machine, electricity usage will also increase proportionately. Rate increases can often be determined by reviewing the utility company's past policy regarding rate increases. In addition, rate increases must usually be approved by the regulatory agencies well in advance of their implementation. Such proceedings are usually published in local papers and trade journals.

For purposes of our forecast, let's assume MBL has projected a 15% rate increase effective August 19X1. The schedule shown in Table 7-10 can then be used to project utility costs.

Table 7-10

MBL Mfg. Co.

Projected Utility Costs for 19X1

Month	Total 19X0	19X0 Factory Portion	Usage Increase	Rate Increase	19X1 Factory Portion	19X0 Other Portion	Rate Increase	19X1 Other Portion
January	$ 900	$600	3%	—	$ 618	$ 300	—	$ 300
February	875	569	3%	—	586	306	—	306
March	1,200	888	3%	—	915	312	—	312
April	1,250	945	3%	—	973	305	—	305
May	1,190	900	3%	—	927	290	—	290
June	295	100	3%	—	103	195	—	195
July	870	590	3%	—	608	280	—	280
August	865	577	3%	15%	683	288	15%	331
September	890	590	3%	15%	699	300	15%	345
October	880	568	3%	15%	673	312	15%	359
November	820	515	3%	15%	610	305	15%	351
December	808	502	3%	15%	595	306	15%	352
					$7,990			$3,726

The amounts calculated in Table 7-10 can now be posted to the forecasting worksheet (Exhibit 7-1). Remember that the factory portion must be charged to inventory and the other portion must be expensed.

Before preparing detailed schedules for various expense items, we must make a determination as to the materiality of each item to the overall forecast. Since MBL has almost $3 million in sales, it seems somewhat unrealistic to prepare detailed schedules for approximately $15,000 of expenses. As a practical matter, by reviewing 19X0's costs, we could easily eyeball an estimate of $600 per month for factory-related utilities and $300 per month for other utilities. Had we used this approach, factory utilities would have been calculated at $7,200 versus $7,990. Similarly, other utilities would total $3,600 versus $3,726. Differences of $790 and $126, respectively, are quite negligible to MBL's total financial picture.

Sales of Peripheral Goods and Services

In addition to a company's normal line of business, it often sells other goods and services that are only incidental to its business. For example, a lumberyard will sell *by-products* such as wood chips to a landscaping firm. Or a retail company, like Sears, will sell *service contracts* on its appliances. The key is to be aware of these types of sales so that they can be included in the forecast. This can best be accomplished by reviewing past financial statements and by discussing this matter with operations and sales personnel.

Let's assume you have learned that MBL offers a three-year service contract with each of its air-conditioning units sold. The contract sells for $36. Past history has indicated that during the contract life, MBL is required to spend, on the average, $4 after the first 9 months, $8 after 18 months, and $12 after 30 months. In addition, approximately 35% of the customers purchase a contract. At the beginning of 19X1, MBL has the following contracts outstanding:

No. of Contracts	Remaining Months
600	30
585	24
806	20
340	6
2,331	

Schedules should be prepared to calculate cash flow and accounting income over the contract lives. Remember, for accounting purposes, the receipts would be netted against future estimated expenses and the net contract income would either be recorded at the time the contract was sold or amortized over the life of the contract. Let's assume that MBL amortizes contract income over the life of the contract. In that case, the following calculation would be made:

Total contract price		$36
Less: Estimated expenses		
9 mo.	$ 4	
18 mo.	8	
30 mo.	12	(24)
Net contract income		$12

Therefore, $12 would be deferred and $0.33 ($12 ÷ 36 mo.) would be recognized as income on a monthly basis.

The schedules shown in Tables 7-11 and 7-12 compute cash flow on new service contracts.

Table 7-11
MBL Mfg. Co.
Calculation of Service Contracts on 19X1 Sales

Sales Month	Sales Quantity	Contracts Sold (Sales × 35%)	Sales Value of Contracts (Contracts × $36)	Cash Repairs		Accounting Income
January	2,020	707	$ 25,452	$ —	[707 × $.33]	$ 233
February	2,040	714	25,704	—	[714 + 707 × $.33]	469
March	2,061	721	25,956	—	[721 + 714 + 707 × .33]	707
April	2,082	729	26,244	—	[729 + ...]	948
May	2,144	750	27,000	—	[750 + ...]	1,195
June	2,208	773	27,828	—	[773 + ...]	1,450
July	2,274	796	28,656	—	[796 + ...]	1,713
August	2,342	820	29,520	—	[820 + ...]	1,984
September	2,365	828	29,808	—	[828 + ...]	2,257
October	2,389	836	30,096	[707 × 4] 2,828	[836 + ...]	2,533
November	2,413	845	30,420	[714 × 4] 2,856	[845 + ...]	2,812
December	2,437	853	30,708	[721 × 4] 2,884	[853 + ...]	3,093
			$337,392	$8,568		$19,394

Table 7-12

MBL Mfg. Co.

Calculation of Service Contracts on Prior Sales

		Cash Repairs			
Month	Contracts Outstanding	9 mo.	18 mo.	30 mo.	Accounting Income
Jan.	$2,331 (340[a] × $12)			$4,080	$ 769 (2,331 × $.33)
Feb.	2,331 (806[b] × $ 8)		$ 6,448		769
Mar.	2,331 (600[c] × $ 4)	$2,400			769
Apr.	2,331				769
May	2,331				769
June	2,331 (585[d] × $ 8)		4,680		769
July	1,991[e]				657 (1,991 × $.33)
Aug.	1,991				657
Sept.	1,991				657
Oct.	1,991				657
Nov.	1,991				657
Dec.	1,991 (600[f] × $ 8)		4,800		657
		$2,400	$15,928	$4,080	$8,556

[a] 36 mo. − 7 mo. = 29 mo. lapsed/ 29 mo. + 1 mo. = 30 mo. (Jan. 19X1).
[b] 36 mo. − 20 mo. = 16 mo. lapsed/ 16 mo. + 2 mo. = 18 mo. (Feb. 19X1)
[c] 36 mo. − 30 mo. = 6 mo. lapsed/ 6 mo. + 3 mo. = 9 mo. (March 19X1).
[d] 36 mo. − 24 mo. = 12 mo. lapsed/ 12 mo. + 6 mo. = 18 mo. (June 19X1)
[e] $2,331 − 340 expiring in six months.
[f] If 9 months have lapsed in March of 19X0, then 18 months will have lapsed in December 19X1. Thus, the 600 group contracts will require both the 9- and 18-month repairs in 19X1.

Let's now post to the forecasting worksheet (Exhibit 7-1). Remember, for accounting purposes, when the contract is sold, the cash received is recorded as follows:

	Dr	Cr
Cash	$36	
Deferred servicing fee income		$12
Liability under servicing contracts		24

Therefore, of the $337,392 collected, $112,464 ($337,392 × ⅓) would be set up as deferred servicing fee income and $224,928 would be set up as a liability for future service repairs.

The deferred income is amortized into income at $0.33 per month and the cash repairs are charged to the liability account when incurred.

Other Expenses

The best way to determine if there are any other expenditures affecting cash flow is to review past income statements, balance sheets, statements of changes in financial position, and trial balances, and to list any cash expenditures not previously included in your forecast working papers. Once you have identified these items, you should do the following:

- Determine the likelihood of recurrence during the forecast period.
- Determine the timing of the cash and/or income statement impact during the forecast period.
- Identify those factors that are likely to cause increases or decreases in these items.
- Quantify the effect of these factors.
- Prepare an appropriate working paper and post the results to the forecasting worksheet.

Your discussions with company employees may also clue you in to items that may impact cash flow. For example, in discussing sales growth with the sales manager, you may learn that the company is planning a major advertising campaign. In this case, you should quantify these advertising costs and if significant include them in your forecast.

In reviewing and forecasting these "other" items, remember we are *not* preparing audited financial statements. The degree of accuracy required in the forecast should be measured in terms of the time and effort it will take to obtain a "precise" estimate.

Exhibit 7-1
MBL Mfg. Co.
Forecasting Worksheet for the Year Ended 12/31/19X1

	Cash Flow						Income Statement					Balance Sheet						
	Salary and Wages	FIT Payments	FICA Payments	Accounting	Utilities	Service Contract Income	Salary and Wages	FICA	Accounting	Utilities	Service Contracts	Cash	Inventory	FIT and FICA Withholdings	Accounts Payable	Deferred Service Contracts	Liab. Under Service Contracts	Retained Earnings
Salaries:																		
Factory	$(245,337)											$(245,337)	$245,337					
Salesmen	(77,860)						$ (77,860)					(77,860)						$ (77,860)
President	(107,615)						(107,615)					(107,615)						(107,615)
Vice presidents	(207,620)						(207,620)					(207,620)						(207,620)
Exec. vice president	(65,412)						(65,412)					(65,412)						(65,412)
Clerical	(21,615)						(21,615)					(21,615)						(21,615)
New employees	(6,500)						(6,500)					(6,500)						(6,500)
FIT	201,095	$(201,095)										201,095		$ 201,095				
												(201,095)		(201,095)				
FICA	31,050	(62,100)						$(16,012)				31,050	15,038	31,050				(16,012)
												(62,100)		(31,050)				
Accounting				$(32,000)					$(36,000)			(32,000)			$4,000			(36,000)
Utilities					$(11,716)					$(3,726)		(11,716)	7,990					(3,726)
Service contracts:																		
New sales						$337,392					19,394	337,392				$112,464	$224,928	19,394
						(8,568)						(8,568)				(19,394)	(8,568)	
						(2,400)						(2,400)					(2,400)	
						(15,928)						(15,928)					(15,928)	
						(4,080)						(4,080)					(4,080)	
Old sales											8,556					(8,556)		8,556
	$(499,814)	$(263,195)	—	$(32,000)	$(11,716)	$306,416	$(486,622)	$(16,012)	$(36,000)	$(3,726)	$27,950	$(500,309)	$268,365	—	$4,000	$ 84,514	$193,952	$(514,410)

CHAPTER

Compilation of a Total Forecast Package

In the preceding chapters, we reviewed in detail the assumptions necessary to prepare a forecast. Throughout the text, we prepared detailed forecasting worksheets for each area of the forecast. We are now ready to compile the actual forecast and prepare the forecasted statements.

The first step in the compilation process is to summarize each of the forecasting worksheets. The following worksheets are designed to summarize each of the forecasted statements we intend to prepare:

• Balance sheet (See Exhibits 8-1 and 8-2)
• Income statement (See Exhibit 8-3)
• Cash flow statement (See Exhibit 8-4)

It should be noted that in preparing the balance sheet summary, we should begin with the actual (historical) beginning balances for the period to be forecasted.

Once the summary worksheets are prepared, we can prepare formal statements. However, before preparing the actual statements, it is a good idea to summarize the major assumptions made in the forecast. Since these assumptions are so significant to the forecasting process, they should actually be typed and presented with the formal statements. The forecast in this chapter represents an "as is" scenerio and therefore has minimal assumptions incorporated in it. However, regardless of the number, all assumptions should be presented. The following is a sample of the forecast assumptions used to prepare the MBL forecasted statements.

MBL Mfg. Co.
Forecast Assumptions
for the Period Ending 12/31/19X1

The following forecasted financial statements were prepared on an "as is" basis with only minimal capital events programmed. The following assumptions were made throughout the period:

1. Excess cash is kept in a nonearning account and therefore generates no income.
2. Sales grow at a compounded rate as follows:

January–April	1%
May–August	3%
September–December	1%

3. The N.J. Power bond (see Table 3-6) matures on 6/15/19X1 and pays off at face ($300,000).
4. The economic order quantity for wing screws is 2,114 dozen.
5. Prime rate is projected as follows:

January–June	17%
July–September	16%
October–December	14%

6. December receivables of $268,070 are sold to a factor for $260,215 in order to yield 18%.
7. $100,000 of 12% subordinated debentures are redeemed at par in September.

The statements themselves can be prepared in many different formats. Since they are management tools, the format used should be whatever is most meaningful to management. Typically, the balance sheet and income statement forecasts are prepared in the normal financial statement presentation of the company. For example, the income statement of a manufacturing company might begin with gross sales, deducting out cost of goods sold to arrive at a gross profit, while a mortgage finance company may present several classes of revenue to arrive at gross revenue and then deduct all expenses to arrive at net income. In addition, a balance sheet may be classified, depending on industry practice. Tables 8-1 and 8-2 show a sample forecasted balance sheet and a sample forecasted income statement for MBL Manufacturing Company.

On the sample forecasted income statement, you will see a "Provision for Federal Income Taxes." So far, we have not discussed how to calculate this provision. In general the provision can be calculated in two ways.

Table 8-1
MBL Mfg. Co.
Sample Forecasted Balance Sheet as of 12/31/19X1

Assets		
Current Assets:		
Cash		$2,707,616
Short-term Investments (net of unamortized		
discount of $196)		9,804
Accounts Receivable		108,682
Inventory		219,087
Prepaid Expenses and Other Assets		12,255
Total Current Assets		3,057,444
Long-term Assets:		
Investments (net of unamortized discount of		
$14,250)		569,352
Property, Plant, and Equipment	$1,000,000	
Leasehold Improvements	638,000	
Less: Accumulated Depreciation	(412,000)	1,226,000
Total Long-term Assets		1,795,352
Total Assets		$4,852,796

Liabilities and Stockholders' Equity		
Current Liabilities:		
Accounts Payable		$ 504,000
Due to Factors		268,070
Other Current Liabilities		83,000
Total Current Liabilities		855,070
Long-term Liabilities:		
Bank Debt		150,000
Debentures		600,000
Deferred Service Costs and Other Liabilities		682,064
Total Long-term Liabilities		1,432,064
Stockholders' Equity:		
Capital Stock (60,000 shares issued and		
outstanding)		60,000
Paid-in Capital		848,000
Retained Earnings		1,657,662
Total Stockholders' Equity		2,565,662
Total Liabilities and Stockholders' Equity		$4,852,796

Table 8-2

MBL Mfg. Co.

Sample Forecasted Income Statement for the Year
Ended 12/31/19X1

Gross Sales	$3,071,783
Cost of Goods Sold	(1,004,063)
Gross Profit on Sales	2,067,720
Interest Income	246,702
Service Fee Income	27,950
Total Revenues	2,342,372
Operating Expenses:	
Salaries and Benefits	502,634
Interest	135,995
Repairs and Maintenance	41,345
Accounting	36,000
Depreciation	30,000
Utilities	3,726
Other	65,213
Total Expenses	814,913
Income before Provision for Federal Income Taxes	1,527,459
Provision for Federal Income Taxes	683,381
Net Income	$ 844,078

1. Obtain the company's actual average tax rate and apply it to forecasted income before taxes. For example, if MBL's effective tax rate in past years has been 43%, then taxes can be calculated by merely applying the 43% rate to forecasted income before provision for federal income taxes as follows:

$$\begin{array}{r} \$1,527,459 \\ \underline{43\%} \end{array}$$

Provision for Federal Income Taxes: $ 656,807

2. Allocate earnings into either ordinary income or capital gains categories and calculate the tax provisions based on federal income tax rates. Since MBL has no income taxed at capital gains rates, the tax can be calculated as follows:

Tax on	$	25,000 @ 17% = $	4,250
Tax on		25,000 @ 20% =	5,000
Tax on		25,000 @ 30% =	7,500
Tax on		25,000 @ 40% =	10,000
Tax on		1,427,459 @ 46% =	656,631
		$1,527,459	$683,381

After calculating the provision for federal income tax, it is always a good idea to review the tax assumptions with the individual responsible for filing the tax returns. This will ensure that all permanent and timing differences have been considered. In addition, it will verify that estimated tax payments have been made on a quarterly basis, and that the total provision will be paid throughout the year.

Remember that the cash and retained earnings in the forecasted balance sheet must be adjusted for the tax provision as follows:

	Cash	Retained Earnings
Per forecast worksheets	$3,390,997	$2,341,043
Tax payments	(683,381)	(683,381)
Adjusted balance	$2,707,616	$1,657,662

The cash flow forecast statement, like the balance sheet and income statement, should be presented in whatever format is most beneficial to its users. However, when it comes to cash, the key distinction is not whether the amounts represent income or nonincome cash. Rather, the major consideration is whether there is an inflow or outflow of cash. For example, from a cash flow standpoint, the *amount* of the constant monthly payment (principal and interest) on a mortgage loan is far more important than its financial statement classification. We're more concerned with the amounts of cash outflow than whether the monthly payment is interest expense or a reduction of the debt principal.

The same is true of salary expense. From a cash flow standpoint, there is no difference between the payroll check that goes to the factory worker and the check to the bookkeeper. Consequently, in presenting cash flow statements, it is often helpful to break down cash flow receipts and disbursements based on their predictibility or repetitiveness. Thus, we can break down the cash flow statement into two components:

1. *Operating receipts and disbursements.* These would include regular *recurring* items that are required to run an ongoing business. For example:
   a. Collections on accounts receivable
   b. Required debt payments (principal and interest)
   c. Repairs and maintenance
   d. Wages and benefits
   e. Insurance
   f. Interest
2. *Nonoperating receipts and disbursements.* These would include receipts and disbursements made at management's option, sometimes called "capital events." These would include, for example:
   a. Long-term borrowings
   b. Investments in mortages, bonds, etc.

c. Purchase of property, plant, and equipment
d. Sales of assets

Table 8-3 is a sample cash flow forecast statement for MBL using the above criteria.

Table 8-3

MBL Mfg. Co.

Sample Forecasted Cash Flow for the Year Ended
12/31/19X1

Operating Receipts:		
Accounts Receivable and Cash		
Sales		$3,441,101
Service Contracts		306,416
Investments*		322,839
Total Operating Receipts		$4,070,356
Operating Disbursements:		
Salaries and Benefits		763,009
Purchase of Inventory		351,785
Interest Payments		73,995
Repairs and Maintenance		41,345
Accounting		32,000
Mortgage Payments		12,000(a)
Utilities		11,716
Lease Payments		2,213
Other		60,800
Tax Payments		683,381
Total Operating Disbursements		2,032,244
Net Operating Cash Flow		2,038,112
Nonoperating:		
Maturity of Municipal Bonds	300,000(b)	
Factoring Proceeds	260,215	
Subordinated Debt Maturity	(100,000)(a)	460,215
Total Increase in Cash		$2,498,327

*Recurring cash flow from investments consist of the following:

Interest	$244,441
Principal on Self-Amortizing Mortgage	16,398(b)
Maturities on Short-Term Investments	62,000(b)
	$322,839

(a)Combined in Exhibit 8-4
(b)Combined in Exhibit 8-4

In addition to the hypothetical forecasted financial statements for MBL, the following examples contain actual cash flow formats used by two companies. These forecasted statement formats were reprinted with the permission of the issuing companies, SMI and TRW. We express our gratitude to these companies for the use of their forecasts.

Example 8-1. Cash Flow Format for SMI Investors (Delaware) Inc.

SMI is currently engaged in the business of financing, investing in, and operating real estate assets. Through a program of business diversification, SMI is seeking to acquire other financial assets and business entities.

The following is a summary of financial highlights obtained from SMI's 1980 annual report:

Total Assets	$94,108,775
Stockholders' Equity	$47,806,832
Net Income	$ 3,581,637

Example 8-1. Cash Flow Format for SMI Investors (Delaware) Inc.

Forecasted Balance Sheet Based on October 16, 1980, Cash Flow Sensitivity
($000s)

	Actual	Pro Forma			
	9/30/80	9/30/81	9/30/82	9/30/83	9/30/84
ASSETS					
Investments in Real Estate					
Mtg. loans: Medical					
Commercial (net of discounts)					
In process of foreclosures					
Operating properties					
Land					
Total investments in real estate	___	___	___	___	___
Accrued interest receivable	___	___	___	___	___
Less allowances for possible losses	___	___	___	___	___
Other Assets					
Receivable from SCC					
Cash and short-term investments, at cost, which approximates market					
Unamortized debt expense					
Deferred charges					
Miscellaneous	___	___	___	___	___
Total Assets					

124

Liabilities

Commercial bank borrowings

Debentures

Senior:

14% due 1987

Less unamortized debt discount

7¾% due 1982

Less unamortized debt discount

Subordinated 6% due 1982

Less unamortized debt discount

Mortgage notes payable

Participations sold in mortgage portfolio

Accrued interest payable and other liabilities

Total liabilities

Stockholders' Equity

Common Stock, $1 par value, 1000 shares authorized

Additional paid in capital

Retained deficit

Total liabilities and stockholder's equity

Example 8-1. Cash Flow Format for SMI Investors (Delaware) Inc.

Forecasted Income Statement as of October 16, 1980

	Twelve Months Ended 9/30/80	Twelve Months Ended 9/30/81	Twelve Months Ended 9/30/82	Twelve Months Ended 9/30/83	Twelve Months Ended 9/30/84
Income					
Commercial Portfolio					
Operating Inc. of REO (Save Inn, Professional Tower & P & M)					
Medical Portfolio					
Home Mortgage Portfolio (serviced by):					
GECC					
Semorco & others					
WFRS					
Other (interest earned on excess cash at 11%)					
Gain on retirement of debentures					
Gain on exchange of debentures					
Gain on sale of real estate					
Interest on SCC note					

Operating
Debt (exclusive of amortization)*
Interest: Revolver
New Debentures 14%
($10M) (8/1/80)
Mischer Debentures
@14% ($2M) (1/1/81)
Depreciation
Amortization of debt discount
Amortization of debt expense
Interest capitalized

Net income (loss)
Effective of 1 point move in prime rate

*Assumes $11,000,000 of bank borrowings draw-down on 4/30/82.

Example 8-1.
Cash Flow Format for SMI Investors (Delaware) Inc.

Cash Flow Forecast & Sensitivity Analysis as of October 16, 1980 ($000s)

	Twelve Months Ended 9/30/80	Seven Months Ended 4/30/81	Twelve Months Ended 9/30/81	Seven Months Ended 4/30/82	Twelve Months Ended 9/30/82	Twelve Months Ended 9/30/82	Twelve Months Ended 9/30/84
RECEIPTS							
Commercial Portfolio							
Operating Income of REO (Save Inn)							
Medical Portfolio							
Home Mortgage Portfolio (serviced by):							
GECC							
Semorco & others							
WFRS							
Sales, repayments and miscellaneous receipts	——	——	——	——	——	——	——
TOTAL RECEIPTS	——	——	——	——	——	——	——
DISBURSEMENTS							
Operating expenses							
Debt expenses (exclusive of amortization)							
Other operating payments (RE taxes & mortgages)							
Commission payments for lots sold (Lake Riverside)							
Principal payments on participations sold							
Principal payments on real estate liens							
TOTAL DISBURSEMENTS	——	——	——	——	——	——	——
NET CASH FLOW FROM OPERATIONS)							

I. Actual
Barlovento
Michigan Class Action Settlement
Sandpiper (Settlement B. Glass)
Doctors Hospital
GECC Participation
Las Palmas Apts. & Buena Vista Land
Second Dimension Apts.
Camelot Manor Mobile Home Pk.
Ramapo Hospital
Dyckman Apts.
Professional Tower—Office
Washington Hospital (assumption fee)
Parker Deauville Apts.

II. Contractual
Las Palmas Apts. & Buena Vista Land
Grand Concourse Apts.
Unionport Road
Rosjean Realty
32155 Broadway
J. Clarence Davies
Snell Eden Isle
Urbanetics Apts. (#3)

III. Forecasted
Washington Hospital
Creekside
Regional Land
Save Inn Motel
Urbanetics Apts. (#13)
Urbanetics Apts. (#6)
Westwood Plaza Off. Bldg. & Rec. Fac.
Sioux City Land
Chappaquonsett Land
Squire Valley

Example 8-1.

Cash Flow Format for SMI Investors (Delaware) Inc.

Cash Flow Forecast & Sensitivity Analysis as of October 16, 1980 (Cont.)

	Twelve Months Ended 9/30/80	Seven Months Ended 4/30/81	Twelve Months Ended 9/30/81	Seven Months Ended 4/30/82	Twelve Months Ended 9/30/82	Twelve Months Ended 9/30/82	Twelve Months Ended 9/30/84
III. Forecasted (cont.)							
Beverly Manor Hospital PLB & MTG							
Commercial Land							
Beefsteak Charlie's Rest.							
Sheraton Concord Hotel							
Sale GECC Participation							
Tallahassee Land							
Pinon Hills							
	___	___			___	___	___
Total sources of cash Comm/Medical Port.							
Effects of loans/investments sold or paid-off							
Expenses of Exchange Offer							
Purchase S & L (1/1/81)							
Drawdown of Revolver 4/30/82							
Expenses SCC & SMI Reorganization							
Paydown of Revolver							
Debenture Exchange ($10 M applied to 1981 Final Maturity)							
Interest: Revolver							
New debentures @ 14% ($10M exchange)							
Mischer Debentures @ 14% ($2M)							
Interest income SCC note (BFSA)							
Reinvestment of excess cash @ 11%							
	___	___			___	___	___
Net Cash Flow							
Debenture Purchases							
Net Cash Flow after Debenture Purchases							
Cumulative Cash Flow							
Bank Debt Outstanding							

Example 8-2. Cash Flow Format for TRW, Inc.

TRW is a multinational company with $5 billion dollars of sales in the car and truck, electronics and space systems, and industrial and energy areas.

The following is a summary of financial highlights obtained from TRW's 1980 annual report:

Total Assets	$2,854,699,000
Stockholders' Equity	$1,287,108,000
Net Income	$ 211,890,000
Shares Outstanding	$ 32,010,000
Primary Earnings Per Share	$ 6.39

Illustrative Balance Sheet Forecast

	Actual		Forecast
	12/31/79	12/31/80	12/31/81
NET DEBT REQUIRED			
Current Assets:			
Accounts Receivable	$	$	$
Inventories			
Prepaid Expenses			
Total Current Assets			
Less Current Operating Liabilities			
Accounts Payable			
Payroll and Other Accruals			
Income Tax Accrual			
Total Current Liabilities			
OPERATING WORKING CAPITAL			
Fixed Assets:			
Property, Plant, and Equipment			
Equipment Mfg. for Lease			
Investment in Associated Companies			
Intangibles			
Other Assets			
Total Fixed Assets			
Less: Deferred Taxes			
Minority Interest			
OPERATING INVESTMENT REQUIRED			
Less: Shareholders' Investment			
Dividends Payable			
NET DEBT REQUIRED			
COMPOSITION OF NET DEBT:			
Debt (b)			
Normal Cash			
Securities			
Net Debt	$	$	$
CAPITAL STRUCTURE RATIOS:			
Debt/Total Capital			
Debt/Total Capital if Securities Were Used to Retire Debt			
Debt/Equity			
Debt/Equity if Securities Were Used to Retire Debt			

Example 8-2.
Cash Flow Format for TRW, Inc.

Illustrative Cash Flow Forecast

	Actual	Forecast
	1980	**1981**
SOURCES		
Net Income	$	$
Depreciation		
Deferred Taxes		
Total Sources		
REQUIREMENTS—FAVORABLE (UNFAVORABLE)		
Capital Expenditures		
Dividends Paid		
Changes in Operating Working Capital:		
Accounts Receivable—(Inc)—Dec.		
Inventories—(Inc)—Dec.		
Prepaid Expenses—(Inc)—Dec.		
Accounts Payable—Inc—(Dec)		
Payroll and Other Accruals—Inc—(Dec)		
Current Income Taxes—Inc—(Dec)		
Total Working Capital Changes		
All Other		
Total Requirements		
TOTAL CASH EXCESS (SHORTAGE)		
REPRESENTED BY CHANGES IN:		
Normal Cash		
Marketable Securities		
Debt		
Total		

Exhibit 8-1

MBL Mfg Co.

Balance Sheet Forecasting Worksheet for the Year Ended 12/31/19X1

Assets

	(a) Cash	Accounts Receivable	(a) Savings Account	(b) Long-Term Investments	(c) Short-Term Investments	(b) Unamortized Discount	(c) Unamortized Discount	Accrued Interest Receivable	Inventory	PP & E	Leaseholds	Accumulated Depreciation	(d) Prepaid Insurance	(d) Deferred Int. Exp.
Balance Beginning Year	$ 200,000	$478,000	$10,560	$ 900,000	$ 70,000	$(15,000)	$(1,175)	$ 197	$ 103,000	$1,000,000	$638,000	$(382,000)	$ 6,600	
Exhibit 2-1	3,446,051	(369,318)	(1,271)	(316,398)	(60,000)	750	979	(197)						
Exhibit 3-1	617,889													
Exhibit 4-1	(351,785)								(152,278)					
Exhibit 5-1	(104,358)											(30,000)	(2,200)	
Exhibit 6-1	74,220								268,365					$7,855
Exhibit 7-1	(500,309)							—						
	$3,381,708	$ 108,682	$ 9,289	$ 583,602	$ 10,000	$(14,250)	$(196)		$ 219,087	$1,000,000	$638,000	$(412,000)	$ 4,400	$7,855

Note: Letters indicate balance sheet groupings.

133

Exhibit 8-2
MBL Mfg. Co.
Balance Sheet Forecasting Worksheet for the Year Ended 12/31/19X1
Liabilities and Stockholders' Equity

	Retained Earnings	Accounts Payable	(a) Mortgages Payable	(a) Interest Payable	Debentures	Factoring Liability	FITA and FICA Withholdings	Bank Loans	(b) Deferred Service Contract	(b) Liab. Under Service Contract	Capital Stock	Paid in Surplus
Balance Beginning Year	$ 813,584		$ 25,000	$ 8,000	$ 700,000			$150,000	$163,848	$239,750	$60,000	$848,000
Exhibit 2-1	3,076,733											
Exhibit 3-1	241,752											
Exhibit 4-1	(1,004,063)	$500,000										
Exhibit 5-1	(136,558)					$268,070						
Exhibit 6-1	(135,995)		(12,000)	62,000	(100,000)							
Exhibit 7-1	(514,410)	4,000							84,514	193,952		
	$ 2,341,043	$504,000	$ 13,000	$70,000	$ 600,000	$268,070		$150,000	$248,362	$433,702	$60,000	$848,000

Note: Letters indicate balance sheet groupings.

Exhibit 8-3
MBL Mfg. Co.
Income Statement Forecasting Worksheet for the Year Ended 12/31/19X1

	Sales	Interest Income	Cost of Goods Sold	Repairs and Maintenance	Other	Depreciation	Interest Expense	(a) Salary and Wages	(a) FICA	Accounting	Utilities	Service Contract Income
Exhibit 2-1	$3,071,783	$ 4,950										
Exhibit 3-1		241,752										
Exhibit 4-1			$(1,004,063)									
Exhibit 5-1				$(41,345)	$(65,213)	$(30,000)	$(135,995)					
Exhibit 6-1								$(486,622)	$(16,012)	$(36,000)	$(3,726)	$27,950
Exhibit 7-1	$3,071,783	$246,702	$(1,004,063)	$(41,345)	$(65,213)	$(30,000)	$(135,995)	$(486,622)	$(16,012)	$(36,000)	$(3,726)	$27,950

Note: Letters indicate income statement groupings.

Exhibit 8-4
MBL Mfg. Co.
Cash Flow Statement Forecasting Worksheet for the Year Ended 12/31/19X1

	(a) Sales	(a) Collections On Accounts Receivable	Interest Income	Inventory	Repairs and Maintainance	Lease Payments	Other Payments	Interest Payments	Principal Payments	Proceeds From Factoring	(b) Salary and Wages	(b) FTT Payments	FICA Payments	Accounting	Utilities	Service Contracts	Principal Receipts
Exhibit 2-1	$237,500	$3,203,601	$ 4,950														$378,398
Exhibit 3-1			239,491	$(351,785)													
Exhibit 4-1					$(41,345)	$(2,213)	$(60,800)										
Exhibit 5-1								$(73,995)	$(112,000)	$260,215							
Exhibit 6-1											$(499,814)	$(263,195)	--	$(32,000)	$(11,716)	$306,416	
Exhibit 7-1																	
	$237,500	$3,203,601	$244,441	$(351,785)	$(41,345)	$(2,213)	$(60,800)	$(73,995)	$(112,000)	$260,215	$(499,814)	$(263,195)	--	$(32,000)	$(11,716)	$306,416	$378,398

Note: Letters indicate cash flow statement groupings.

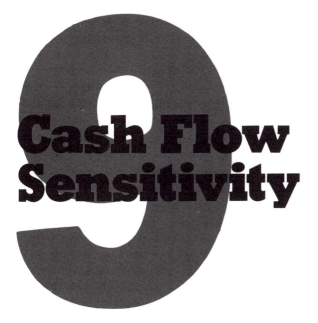

Cash Flow Sensitivity

As we have mentioned throughout the text, the most important feature of a cash flow forecast is its ability to answer a series of "what if" questions. Before continuing with MBL's sensitivity analysis, let us expand the existing "as is" one-year cash flow to a three-year projection. This can be done by making several modifications to the existing assumptions:

1. Review existing assumptions in the "as is" forecast and change assumptions, when appropriate. In today's constantly changing interest rate environment, last week's assumptions may be outdated and no longer valid. Therefore, all assumptions should be reviewed and modified as required. This is true even if we are only reissuing previous "as is" forecasts.

2. Conservatively estimate sales growth. Sales growth is the function of two factors: increased sales and increased sales prices. Since there usually is both a point of market saturation and a manufacturing capacity limit, which both limit sales growth, it is usually a good idea to be conservative and allow sales growth to level off in a long-range forecast. Remember, additional sales can always be programmed into the "what if" scenario.

3. Keep interest rate changes to a minimum. Instead you should try to use one rate throughout the forecast and consider rate changes in the "what if" scenario.

4. Use a suspense account for long-term bonds and debt. The longer the forecast period, the more likely it is that long-term bonds or debt will mature. It is therefore often best to permit the funds that flow from these activities to accumulate in a nonearning "excess/deficit" account to be dealt with in the "what if" scenario.

5. Program increases in selected expenses. Certain expenses such as salaries and wages should have forecasted increases since such expenses are rarely, if ever, reduced (one exception is through a contraction of the business).

Let's now look at Table 9-1, a basic three-year forecast for MBL. We can use this forecast as a starting point from which we will forecast several sensitivity assumptions.

Table 9-1

MBL Mfg. Co.

Forecasted Cash Flow for the Three Years Ending 12/31

	19X1	19X2	19X3
Operating Receipts:			
Accounts Receivable and Cash Sales	$3,441,101	$3,246,040	$3,464,381
Service Contracts	306,416	330,000	342,618
Investments	322,839	284,650	290,432
Total Operating Receipts	4,070,356	3,860,690	4,097,431
Operating Disbursements:			
Salaries and Benefits	763,009	846,832	987,481
Purchases of Inventory	351,785	952,830	937,800
Interest Payments	73,995	52,864	46,438
Repairs and Maintenance	41,345	48,780	52,817
Accounting	32,000	34,000	37,000
Mortgage Payments	12,000	13,000	—
Utilities	11,716	12,486	16,483
Lease Payments	2,213	2,213	2,213
Tax Payments	683,381	724,861	847,932
Other	60,800	62,000	68,000
Total Operating Disbursements	2,032,244	2,749,866	2,996,164
Net Operating Cash Flow	2,038,112	1,110,824	1,101,267
Nonoperating:			
Bond Maturities	300,000	—	—
Factoring Proceeds (Payments)	260,215	(260,215)	—
Debt Maturities	(100,000)	(100,000)	(500,000)
Total Excess (Deficit)	$2,498,327	$ 750,609	$ 601,276

Changes in Interest Rates

One of the most frequently asked "what if" questions concerns changes in interest rates. This is especially true in highly rate-sensitive environments where either a major portion of the company's debt is tied to the prime rate (for example, the interest on the borrowing is at prime plus 2 points) or older "below market" rate debt is coming due and must be replaced with new current-rate debt.

The best way to approach the issue of debt tied to the prime rate is to prepare a schedule of rate-sensitive debt which lists the amounts of the debt, the existing interest rate, and interest and principal payments. Once this summary is prepared, the effect of rate movements can be easily forecasted. Keep in mind that increases in borrowing rates usually have several economic effects on a company. For example, increased rates may cause sluggish sales and therefore reduce gross profits. For purposes of answering the "what if" rate question, this effect can usually be ignored. We are more interested in determining the "pure" effect of a change in rate on interest expense. For example, if our forecasts projected a 14% prime rate and the prime rate increased to 18%, what would be the effect on interest expense? To illustrate, let's review Table 9-2, a summary of MBL's rate-sensitive debt throughout the three-year forecast period.

Naturally, the effect of a 2-point move in the prime rate will be double

Table 9-2

MBL Mfg. Co.

Summary of Rate-Sensitive Debt for the Three-Year Period Ended 12/31

Type of Debt	Period	Principal Outstanding	Rate	Number of Months	Interest Payments	Interest with 1-point Increase in Prime Rate
19X1						
Renegotiable debt	1/1/19X1-6/30/19X1	$ 50,000	12%	6	$ 3,000	$ 3,000
Renegotiable debt	7/1/19X1-12/31/19X1	50,000	16% + 3%	6	4,750	5,000
Revolving credit	1/1/19X1-6/30/19X1	100,000	17% + 2%	6	9,500	10,000
Revolving credit	7/1/19X1-9/30/19X1	100,000	16% + 2%	3	4,500	4,750
Revolving credit	10/1/19X1-12/31/19X1	100,000	14% + 2%	3	4,000	4,250
					$25,750	$27,000
		Effect of 1-point increase in prime rate:				$1,250
19X2						
Renegotiable debt	1/1/19X2-12/31/19X2	$ 50,000	16% + 3%	12	$ 9,500	$10,000
Revolving credit	1/1/19X2-6/30/19X2	100,000	14% + 2%	6	8,000	8,500
Revolving credit	7/1/19X2-12/31/19X2	400,000	15% + 2%	6	34,000	36,000
					$51,500	$54,500
		Effect of 1-point increase in prime rate:				$3,000
19X3						
Renegotiable debt	1/1/19X3-12/31/19X3	$ 50,000	15% + 2%	12	$ 8,500	$ 9,000
Revolving credit	1/1/19X3-9/30/19X3	400,000	15% + 2%	9	51,000	54,000
Revolving credit	10/1/19X3-12/31/19X3	200,000	15% + 2%	3	8,500	9,000
					$68,000	$72,000
		Effect of 1-point increase in prime rate:				$4,000

the effect of a 1-point move, a 3-point move in the prime rate will be triple
the effect of a 1-point move, etc. A simple approach that can be used to
present this type of sensitivity is to add a one-line presentation to the "as
is" scenario, as shown in Table 9-3.

The effect on the prime rate shown in Table 9-3 is minimal since MBL
has only a small amount of rate-sensitive debt. However, for a company
with $3 million of rate-sensitive debt outstanding, a 1-point move in the
prime rate would cost $30,000.

Table 9-3

MBL Mfg. Co.

Forecasted Cash Flow for the Three Years Ending 12/31

	19X1	19X2	19X3
Operating Receipts:			
Accounts Receivable and Cash Sales	$3,441,101	$3,246,040	$3,464,381
Service Contracts	306,416	330,000	342,618
Investments	322,839	284,650	290,432
Total Operating Receipts	4,070,356	3,860,690	4,097,431
Operating Disbursements:			
Salaries and Benefits	763,009	846,832	987,481
Purchasing of Inventory	351,785	952,830	937,800
Interest Payments	73,995	52,864	46,438
Repairs and Maintenance	41,345	48,780	52,817
Accounting	32,000	34,000	37,000
Mortgage Payments	12,000	13,000	—
Utilities	11,716	12,486	16,483
Lease Payments	2,213	2,213	2,213
Tax Payments	683,381	724,861	847,932
Other	60,800	62,000	68,000
Total Operating Disbursements	2,032,244	2,749,866	2,996,164
Net Operating Cash Flow	2,038,112	1,110,824	1,101,267
Nonoperating:			
Bond Maturities	300,000	—	—
Factoring Proceeds (Payments)	260,215	(260,215)	—
Debt Maturities	(100,000)	(100,000)	(500,000)
Total Excess (Deficit)	$2,498,327	$750,609	$601,267
Effect of a 1-point move in the prime rate	$1,250	$3,000	$4,000

For all companies with large quantities of debt issued several years
back when interest rates were significantly below today's rates, there is a
significant effect when the debt is rolled over at new current rates. To
quantify this effect, a schedule of expected debt maturities, with the old
interest payments, should be prepared. Since the old debt may be at varying rates and may be rolled over at the same time, we cannot talk in terms
of a 1-point increase. For example, if 6% and 10% debentures must be
reissued at 15%, there is a 9% (15% − 6%) and a 5% (15% − 10%) effect,

respectively. In this situation it is best to forecast the new debt at a specific current rate and then analyze 1-point moves in the prime rate.

To illustrate, MBL has the following debt maturities:

Type of Debt	Maturity Date	Current Rate	Principal Amount	Effect of New Debt at 15%			Effect of a 1-Point Move		
				19X1	19X2	19X3	19X1	19X2	19X3
Senior debentures	7/1/19X3	8%	$500,000	$ —	$ —	$17,500	$—	$ —	$2,500
Subordinate debts	9/30/19X1	12%	100,000	750	3,000	3,000	250	1,000	1,000
Subordinate debts	9/30/19X2	12%	100,000	—	750	3,000	—	250	1,000
				$ 750	$3,750	$23,500	$250	$1,250	$4,500

Disclosure of this change in interest can often be easily accomplished by amending the assumption summary sheet. For example:

MBL has long-term debt maturing at varying times throughout the forecast period. Such debt is below current market rates and if it were renewed at a rate of 15%, it would decrease cash flow as follows:

19X1	$ 750
19X2	3,750
19X3	23,500

A 1-point move in the rate above or below the 15% projected level would increase or decrease the above cash flow adjustments as follows:

19X1	$ 250
19X2	1,250
19X3	4,500

Changes in Sales Forecast

As we discussed earlier, sales can be affected by two factors:

1. Change in selling prices
2. Change in sales volume

A change in selling price can be calculated and presented much like a change in interest rate. A change in sales price may have other economic effects, such as a decrease in sales volume. However, again we are trying to obtain a "pure" effect of a sales price increase and therefore these factors should be ignored.

As we did with debt and interest, let's summarize a $1 increase in sales price for MBL (shown in Table 9-4). Remember that we are forecasting the effect of a $1 increase in sales price on cash collections. Therefore, in applying the unit price to sales value, we must work with the sales value per our "Expected Cash Receipts" schedule (Table 2-3) and not the "Com-

Table 9-4

MBL Mfg. Co.

Summary of Sales for the Three-Year Period Ending 19X3

Period	Unit Sales Price	Sales Value at Unit Sales Price	Effect of a $1 Price Unit Sales Price
19X1			
1/1/19X1–3/31/19X1	$100	$ 612,100	$ 6,121
3/31/19X1–12/31/19X1	110	1,738,440	15,804
		Total effect for 19X1:	$21,925
19X2			
1/1/19X2–6/30/19X2	$110	$1,528,400	$13,894
7/1/19X2–12/31/19X2	115	1,755,300	15,263
		Total effect for 19X2:	$29,157
19X3			
7/1/19X3–12/31/19X3	$115	$3,583,650	$31,162

pounded Sales Value Calculations" schedule (Table 2-1). Also keep in mind that a change in sales price will not affect actual sales of previous periods that are collected in 19X1. Consequently, we will only be working with sales that occurred during the forecast period which will be collected during the forecast period.

The computations shown in Table 9-4 represent the gross effect on sales collections. Although an increase in sales price theoretically should not affect the percentage of sales, returns and allowances, and discounts taken, we must still adjust the amount of returns and allowances and discounts on the new sales value. For the period September through December we have assumed that customers will take a 2% discount. This means ⅓ (four out of twelve months) of the increased sales value is subject to the 2% discount. In addition, sales are subject to a 1% sales return. These adjustments are made as follows:

	19X1	19X2	19X3
Gross effect of $1 increase in sales price	$21,925	$29,157	$31,162
Collections net of sales returns and allowances of 1%	$21,706	$28,864	$30,850
Less 2% discount on approximately ⅓ of collections			
(21,706 ÷ 3 × 2%)	(145)		
(28,864 ÷ 3 × 2%)		(192)	
(30,850 ÷ 3 × 2%)			(206)
Total net collections	$21,561	$28,672	$30,644

Again, this can be simply presented in the same one-line format used with the 1-point move in the prime rate in the cash flow forecast, as is demonstrated in Table 9-5.

Table 9-5

MBL Mfg. Co.

Forecasted Cash Flow for the Three Years Ending 12/31

	19X1	19X2	19X3
Operating Receipts:			
Accounts Receivable and Cash			
Sales	$3,441,101	$3,246,040	$3,464,381
Service Contracts	306,416	330,000	342,618
Investments	322,839	284,650	290,432
Total Operating Receipts	4,070,356	3,860,690	4,097,431
Operating Disbursements:			
Salaries and Benefits	763,009	846,832	987,481
Purchasing of Inventory	351,785	952,830	937,800
Interest Payments	73,995	52,864	46,438
Repairs and Maintenance	41,345	48,780	52,817
Accounting	32,000	34,000	37,000
Mortgage Payments	12,000	13,000	—
Utilities	11,716	12,486	16,483
Lease Payments	2,213	2,213	2,213
Tax Payments	683,381	724,861	847,932
Other	60,800	62,000	68,000
Total Operating Disbursements	2,032,244	2,749,866	2,996,164
Net Operating Cash Flow	2,038,112	1,110,824	1,101,267
Nonoperating:			
Bond Maturities	300,000	—	—
Factoring Proceeds (Payments)	260,215	(260,215)	—
Debt Maturities	(100,000)	(100,000)	(500,000)
Total Excess (Deficit)	$2,498,327	$ 750,609	$ 601,267
Effect of a 1-point move in the prime rate	$1,750	$3,000	$4,000
Effect of a $1 increase in sales price	$21,561	$28,672	$30,644

Measuring the effect of a *change in sales volume* can be accomplished by recalculating sales growth at 1% increase. This can be done as follows:

Starting sales volume	2,000	
4-month growth factor @ 2% (1% + 1% increase)	4.20404	
		8,408
Sales volume at end of month 4	2,208	
4-month growth factor @ 4% (3% + 1% increase)	4.41632	
		9,751
Sales volume at end of month 8	2,583	
2-month growth factor @ 2% (1% + 1% increase)	2.020	
		5,218
Total sales collected		23,377

Since an increase in sales volume has no effect on prior-period sales collected in the current period and current-period sales which will not be collected until the following forecast period, an increase in the November and December 19X1 sales will affect not the 19X1 forecast period but rather the 19X2 forecast period.

This increase in sales volume can either be priced out at the original selling price ($107.50) or adjusted to reflect a price increase. For example:

Total sales collected in 19X1 (reflecting 1% increase in sales volume)	23,377	23,377
Selling price:		
As originally projected	$ 107.50	
Reflecting $1.00 price increase		$ 108.50
Revised sales value	$2,513,027	$2,536,404

Again, if we are forecasting a change in sales value, we must adjust for sales returns and discounts. This can be done as follows:

	At $107.50	At $108.50
Revised sales value	$2,513,027	$2,536,404
Less 1% returns	(25,130)	(25,364)
	2,487,897	2,511,040
Less 2% discount	(49,758)	(50,221)
	$2,438,139	$2,460,819

Purchase of Property, Plant, and Equipment

One of the major purposes of a cash flow forecast, especially a long-term forecast, is to determine the effect of certain capital events, such as the expansion of property, plant, and equipment. In forecasting such an event, you must take into consideration the following items:

1. Initial cash outlay
2. Increased financing costs
3. Depreciation
4. Increased repairs and maintenance
5. Increased operating costs, such as new employees, electrical, heat, etc.
6. Increased sales volume and related costs such as inventory, etc.

To illustrate, let's assume that MBL is considering expanding its current facilities. It intends to purchase a new $6 million factory, paying $1 million in cash, financing the remaining amount with a 20-year self-amortizing mortgage at 14%. At full capacity, the new factory will be able to generate 50,000 air-conditioning units per year. However, because of market penetration, only 7,000 more units can be sold per year. The new factory will require fifteen new people to begin operations and will require three additional people for each additional production run of 7,000 units.

The forecast changes required for the above acquisition should be done step by step for each forecast period. If MBL purchases the facilities in June of 19X1, the following forecast adjustments must be made.

Down Payment. A $1 million down payment is required. Since MBL has excess cash during 19X1, it must be reduced for this purchase.

Debt Service. The building will be financed with a 20-year 14% mortgage. Therefore, we must determine the annual debt service (principal and interest) on the obligation. This can be done as follows:

Amount financed	$5,000,000
Factor for periodic monthly payment	
required to pay off $1 in 20 years at 14%	.012435
Monthly debt service	$ 62,175

Since this factory will be purchased in June, debt service for 19X1 will be $373,050 ($62,175 × 6 months). For 19X2 and 19X3, the total amount of debt service will be $746,100 ($62,175 × 12 months).

Depreciation. If an income statement and a balance sheet are to be prepared, depreciation should be calculated using the appropriate depreciation method used by the company (straight-line, double declining balance, etc.).

Heat, Light, and Power. Like any other forecast assumption, these charges should be reviewed with those individuals responsible for their oversight. For example, if a new factory is built to specifications, estimates of electrical usage, etc., can usually be obtained either from the contractor or directly from the power company. If the facility is to be purchased from an existing owner, prior utility bills can be reviewed. In addition, operations of the current facility can often be extrapolated to form a basis for the new forecast. For example, if a current factory producing 28,000 units required $12,000 per year, $5,000 of which is fixed and $7,000 of which is variable, then an approximate per unit charge of $0.25 can be calculated ($7,000 ÷ 28,000 = $0.25). As a result MBL could adjust its forecast for utility charges as follows:

	19X1	19X2	19X3
Fixed cost	$2,500	$5,000	$5,000
Variable cost			
7,000 units × $0.25 × 1/2 yr.	875	875	875
7,000 units × $0.25		1,750	1,750
7,000 units × $0.25			1,750
	$3,375	$7,625	$9,375

Wages and Benefits. If new employees are to be hired, their annual wages, FICA taxes, and benefits must be forecasted. In our original forecasting process we determined that factory workers currently earn the following:

• Bending machine operators—$210 per week
• Drill press operators—$230 per week
• Assemblers—$160 per week

We have also forecasted an annual 6% salary increase in September for factory workers. Remember that these assumptions must be checked to

Table 9-6
MBL Mfg. Co.
*Forecast of Changes in Wages and Benefits Assuming
Purchase of New Factory*

19X1

2 bending machine operators @ $210 per week =	$ 420	
3 drill press operators @ $230 per week =	690	
10 assemblers @ $160 per week =	1,600	
Total weekly salary	$2,710	
Weeks at above salary level	8	
		21,680
Total weekly salary	$2,710	
6% salary increase	106%	
	$2,873	
Weeks at increased salary level (Sept.-Dec.)	18	
		51,714
Total Forecasted Increase for 19X1		$73,394

Table 9-6   (Cont.)

19X2		
Base salary for 15 employees	$2,873	
Weeks until next salary increase (Jan.–Sept)	36	
		103,428
Total weekly salary	$2,873	
6% salary increase	106%	
	$3,045	
Weeks at increased salary level (Sept.–Dec.)	16	
		48,720
3 new assemblers (due to 7,000 volume increase)		
Base salary (June–Sept.) ($2,873 ÷ 15 × 3)	$ 574	
Weeks until next salary increase (June–Sept.)	16	
		9,184
Total weekly salary for new employees	574	
6% salary increase	106%	
	$ 608	
Weeks at increased salary level (Sept.–Dec.)	16	
		9,728
Total salary for 19X2		$171,060

ensure they are still valid. Assuming they are, we need only determine the type of employee that will be required and then we can prepare our forecast adjustments as shown in Table 9-6.

A salary forecast for 19X3 could be prepared using the same format as that shown in Table 9-6, again keeping in mind that any expected salary increase and the three new employees required when the next 7,000-unit production level is achieved must be programmed. Without performing the detailed salary calculations, let's assume that salary expense for 19X3 is $204,000.

The forecasted FICA calculation for MBL is easy because all of the new employees, even with projected salary increases, fall below the maximum FICA levels. Therefore, the FICA withholding percentage can simply be applied to total gross wages as follows:

	19X1	19X2	19X3
Forecasted gross wages	$73,394	$171,060	$204,000
FICA rate	6.13%	6.65%	6.70%
Total FICA	$ 4,499	$ 11,375	$ 13,668

Remember that the FICA rate can only be applied to total gross wages if all salaries within the wages fall below the FICA limit. Carefully review projected salaries, including salary increases, to determine if any employees within the group will meet the FICA limit. If this occurs, FICA should only be calculated on wages up to the limit.

Increased Sales. One of the major concerns when production facilities are expanded is the ability of the market to absorb the increased productivity. The mere ability of a new factory to generate 50,000 units does not guarantee that these units can be sold. Therefore, it is essential to review with marketing and sales personnel the incremental number of units that can be sold at the expected selling price. This last item, expected selling price, is important because sales prices are sometimes lowered in order to provide an incentive for the market to absorb the increased productivity. In our case, MBL has determined that the market is capable of absorbing

Table 9-7

MBL Mfg. Co.

Forecast of Changes in Projected Collections
Assuming Purchase of New Factory

19X1

Total projected sales (½ yr.)	3,500 units
Selling price	$ 107.50
Total sales	$ 376,250
Less: 1% sales return	(3,762)
	372,488
Less: 2% discount	(7,450)
Total collections	$ 365,038

19X2

Total projected sales (7,000 units + 3,500 units)	10,500 units
Selling price	$ 107.50
Total sales	$1,128,750
Less: 1% sales return	(11,287)
	1,117,463
Less: Nov. and Dec. sales requiring 60 days for collection and collected in 19X2 ($1,117,463 ÷ 12 × 2)	(186,244)
Total 19X2 collections	$ 931,219

19X3

Total projected sales (14,000 units + 3,500 units)	17,500 units
Selling price	$ 107.50
Total sales	$1,881,250
Less: 1% sales return	(18,812)
	1,862,438
Less: Oct., Nov., and Dec. sales requiring 90 days for collection and collected in 19X4 ($1,862,438 ÷ 12 × 3)	(465,609)
	1,396,829
Add: 19X2 sales collected in 19X3	186,244
Total 19X3 collections	$1,583,073

only 7,000 new units per year. We can now program our cash flow adjustments for the anticipated production. We must estimate whether or not customers will pay within 10 days and take a 2% discount or take a full 60 days to pay. For illustrative purposes, let's assume that for 19X1 collections will be made within 10 days and a 2% discount will be taken. However, for 19X2 and 19X3 collections will take 60 and 90 days, respectively, and consequently no discount will be taken. As a result, MBL's cash flow collections can be programmed as shown in Table 9-7.

Increased Production. Since we are, in essence, starting production from scratch and are programming production increases, our first step in calculating purchase requirements is to determine the safety stock requirements at each level of production. One way of doing this is by determining the percentage of current safety stock requirements to monthly production and applying that percentage to forecasted production increases. For example, if MBL requires 18% of its monthly production to be maintained as safety stock, we can assume that this inventory will be purchased at the beginning of each forecasted production increase. To illustrate:

Date of Production Increases	Amount of Monthly Production Increase	Safety Stock @ 18%
June 30, 19X1	583	105
June 30, 19X2	583	105
June 30, 19X3	583	105

Once we have determined the required safety stock, we can calculate production requirements based on required lead time. Although detailed production schedules can be prepared, for a long-range forecast it is usually sufficient to use averages and estimates. If MBL requires an average lead time of 24 days, we can calculate assuming that inventory must be purchased 30 days prior to production (24 days lead time plus a 6-day margin for error). Consequently, inventory purchase quantities can be calculated as shown in Table 9-8.

Table 9-8

MBL Mfg. Co.

*Forecast of Changes in Projected Inventory
Purchase Quantities Assuming Purchase of
New Factory*

19X1	
Units to be produced in 19X1 (July–Dec.)	3,500
One month inventory required for lead time	
(3,500 ÷ 6 months)	583
Safety stock	105
Total units to be purchased in 19X1	4,188

Table 9-8 (Cont.)

19X2	
Units to be produced (7,000 × 6/12 months plus 14,000 × 6/12 months)	10,500
One month inventory required for lead time (year end production of 14,000 ÷ 12 months)	1,167
Increase in safety stock	105
Total units to be purchased in 19X2	11,772

19X3	
Units to be produced (14,000 × 6/12 months plus 21,000 × 6/12 months)	17,500
One month inventory required for lead time (year-end production of 21,000 ÷ 12 months)	1,750
Increase in safety stock	105
Total units to be purchased in 19X3	19,355

After calculating the required purchase quantities, we must then price out the purchases, making the appropriate adjustments for price increases. Assuming that prices are expected to rise by 10% in 19X2 and 19X3, inventory purchases can be calculated as follows:

	19X1	19X2	19X3
Units to be purchased	4,188	11,772	19,355
Purchase costs	$ 20.60		
($20.60 × 110%)		$ 22.66	
($22.66 × 110%)			$ 24.93
Total purchases	$86,272	$266,754	$482,520

Income Tax Payments. If detailed adjusted income forecasting worksheets are prepared, they can be used to calculate tax payments. However, if a forecasted income statement is not being prepared for these adjustments, the tax effect of the changes may be calculated and added or deducted from the "as is" tax payments. This can be done as shown in Table 9-9.

Table 9-9
MBL Mfg. Co.
Forecast of Changes in Income Tax Payments Assuming Purchase of New Factory

	19X1	19X2	19X3
Interest on mortgage	($349,227)	($693,366)	($685,491)
Depreciation (assuming 40-year straight line)	(75,000)	(150,000)	(150,000)
Heat, light, and power	(3,375)	(7,625)	(9,375)
Salary	(73,394)	(171,060)	(204,000)

Table 9-9 (Cont.)

	19X1	19X2	19X3
FICA	(4,499)	(11,375)	(13,668)
Sales	365,038	1,117,463	1,862,438
Cost of goods sold			
(3,500 @ 20.60)	(72,100)		
(10,500 @ 22.66)		(237,930)	
(17,500 @ 24.93)			(436,275)
	(212,557)	(153,893)	363,629
Tax rate	46%	46%	46%
Incremental tax payment	(97,776)	(70,790)	167,268

Preparing the "What If" Cash Flow

Once the detailed calculations have been prepared for our new set of assumptions (i.e., purchasing a new factory, etc.) we are ready to post to a revised set of forecasting worksheets. A separate worksheet should be prepared for each year to be forecasted. (See Exhibits 9-1 through 9-3.) The worksheets begin with the balances per the "as is" cash flow. These balances are then adjusted by posting the detailed forecasting assumptions.

In preparing the "as is" and "what if" forecasts, we allowed each to increase or decrease, depending on our assumptions. These increases/ decreases were merely added to or reduced from our cash balances. Since good cash management requires maximum earnings on investments, these funds would, in reality, be invested to achieve the maximum returns on capital. There are several ways of achieving this goal:

1. Assume that all excess funds are used to reduce any outstanding revolving credit lines. Typically, these lines are at the most expensive interest rates. Consequently, their reductions will maximize earnings.
2. Assume that all excess cash will earn interest at current short-term interest rates. This is the most conservative approach since these rates are usually the lowest rates available.
3. Assume that all excess funds are invested in specific investments that are timed to mature when the company needs the cash (for example, the purchase of long-term bonds).
4. Assume that any cash deficiencies are made up by short-term borrowings. Since these rates are usually the highest rates paid, this too is a very conservative approach. However, care should be exercised in evaluating whether this is a realistic assumption. There may not be funds available to the company. For example, if the company has a $600,000 revolving credit line and is projecting a $2 million cash deficit, it may have serious liquidity problems.
5. Program any specific financing arrangements that the company may, in reality, use to fund such deficits; for example, a long-term bond offering or new bank lines.

Calculating a return (expense) on excess (deficit) cash can be done by obtaining an average excess/deficit balance outstanding (balance at the beginning of the period and balance at the end of the period ÷ 2) and applying the appropriate interest rates. This method is used when cash flows are relatively stable throughout the forecast period. Another alternative is to calculate the return (expense) for major events and then use an average balance for the rest of the period.

Let's assume that MBL will use its excess cash to first pay down its revolving credit lines and second to invest at current short-term rates. A good rule of thumb to follow in selecting interest rates is to use prime *less* 1 point for short-term investments of excess cash and prime *plus* 2 points or the company's revolving credit rates, if there are long-term commitments. MBL's excess cash in three successive years and its investment of excess cash are presented in the following tables.

19X1		
Total excess cash assuming purchase of new facility (Exhibit 9-1)		$1,420,551
Add (deduct) events to be handled separately:		
Bond maturities	($300,000)	
Factory proceeds	(260,215)	
Debt maturities	100,000	
Deposit on factory	1,000,000	539,785
Excess retained ratably throughout the year		1,960,336
To average		÷ 2
Average excess to be invested in 19X1		$ 980,168

Table 9-10

MBL Mfg. Co.

Investment of Excess Cash 19X1

Source/Use	Type of Investment	Amount	Rate	No. of Months	Earnings
Operations (average excess: $100,000 + $880,168 = $980,168)	Paydown revolver at prime plus 2 points	$ 100,000	17 + 2	6	$ 9,500
	Paydown revolver at prime plus 2 points	100,000	16 + 2	3	4,500
	Paydown revolver at prime plus 2 points	100,000	14 + 2	3	4,000
	Certificate of deposit at prime minus 1 point	880,168	17 − 1	6	70,413
	Certificate of deposit at prime minus 1 point	880,168	16 − 1	3	33,006
	Certificate of deposit at prime minus 1 point	880,168	14 − 1	3	28,605
Purchase of building (June 30, 19X1)	Certificate of deposit at prime minus 1 point	(1,000,000)	16 − 1	3	(37,500)

Table 9-10 (Cont.)

Source/Use	Type of Investment	Amount	Rate	No. of Months	Earnings
	Certificate of deposit at prime minus 1 point	(1,000,000)	14 − 1	3	(32,500)
Debt maturity (Sept. 19X1)	Certificate of deposit at prime minus 1 point	(100,000)	14 − 1	3	(3,250)
N.J. Power maturity (June 15, 19X1)	Certificate of deposit at prime minus 1 point	300,000	16 − 1	½	1,731
	Certificate of deposit at prime minus 1 point	300,000	14 − 1	3	9,750
Factoring proceeds (Dec. 31. 19X1)	Certificate of deposit at prime minus 1 point	260,215	14 − 1	—	—
					88,255
Less taxes at 46%					(40,597)
			Income earned on excess cash		$ 47,658

. 19X2

Total excess cash assuming purchase of new facility (Exhibit 9-2)		$549,704
Add (deduct) events to be handled separately:		
Payment of factoring proceeds	$260,215	
Debt maturities	$100,000	360,215
Excess received ratably throughout the year		909,919
To average		÷ 2
Average excess to be invested in 19X2		$454,960

Table 9-11

MBL Mfg. Co.

Investment of Excess Cash in 19X2 (Assuming Prime Rate at 14%)

Source/Use	Type of Investment	Amount	Rate	Number of Months	Earnings
19X1 excess cash	Certificate of deposit at prime minus 1 point	$1,420,551	14 − 1	12	$ 184,672
Operations (average excess: $100,000 + $354,960 = $454,960)	Paydown revolver at prime plus 2 points	100,000	14 + 2	12	16,000
	Certificate of deposit at prime minus 1 point	354,960	14 − 1	12	46,145
Factoring payment (Feb. 28, 19X2)	Certificate of deposit at prime minus 1 point	(260,215)	14 − 1	2	(5,638)
Debt maturity (Sept. 19X2)	Certificate of deposit at prime minus 1 point	(100,000)	14 − 1	3	(3,250)
Earnings on 19X1 excess	Certificate of deposit at prime minus 1 point	47,658	14 − 1	12	6,196
					244,125
Less taxes at 46%					(112,297)
			Income earned on excess cash 19X2		$ 131,828

19X3	
Total excess assuming purchase of new facility, (Ex. 9-3)	$ 561,409
Add (deduct) events to be handled separately:	
Debt maturities	500,000
Excess received ratably throughout the year	1,061,409
To average	÷ 2
Average excess to be invested in 19X3	$ 530,705

Table 9-12
MBL Mfg. Co.
Investment of Excess Cash in 19X3
(Assuming Prime Rate at 14% Jan–July and 13% Aug–Dec)

Source/Use	Type of Investment	Amount	Rate	No. of Months	Earnings
19X1 excess cash	Certificate of deposit at prime minus 1 point	$1,420,551	14 − 1	7	$ 107,725
	Certificate of deposit at prime minus 1 point	1,420,551	13 − 1	5	71,028
1982 average excess cash	Certificate of deposit at prime minus 1 point	454,960	14 − 1	7	34,501
	Certificate of deposit at prime minus 1 point	454,960	13 − 1	5	22,748
Operations (Average excess:	Paydown of revolver	100,000	14 + 2	7	9,333
$100,000 + $430,705 =	Paydown of revolver	100,000	13 + 2	5	6,250
$530,705)	Certificate of deposit at prime minus 1 point	430,705	14 − 1	7	32,662
	Certificate of deposit at prime minus 1 point	430,705	13 − 1	5	21,535
Debt maturity (July 1, 19X1)	Certificate of deposit at prime minus 1 point	(500,000)	13 − 1	6	(30,000)
Earnings on 19X1 excess	Certificate of deposit at prime minus 1 point	47,658	14 − 1	7	3,615
	Certificate of deposit at prime minus 1 point	47,658	13 − 1	5	2,383
Earnings on 19X2 excess	Certificate of deposit at prime minus 1 point	131,828	14 − 1	7	9,997
	Certificate of deposit at prime minus 1 point	131,828	13 − 1	5	6,591
					298,368
Less taxes at 46%					(137,249)
		Income earned on excess cash 19X3			$ 161,119

The interest and tax balances obtained in Tables 9-10, 9-11, and 9-12 can now be posted to the cash flow forecasting worksheets (Exhibits 9-1 through 9-3).

Upon completion of this posting, we can prepare our final cash flow statement and revised forecast assumptions for MBL. Here too, these statements can be prepared in various formats. Examples 9-1 and 9-2 show two sample formats for the final cash flow statement.

Example 9-1 incorporates the effects of the new facility within the body of the cash flow statement. Example 9-2 shows the separate effect of the purchase.

However, before preparing the forecast, the assumptions should be summarized for presentation with the forecast.

MBL Mfg. Co.
Forecast Assumptions
for Acquisition of New Facility

1. The new facility is to be purchased in June 19X1 at a cost of $6,000,000:

Cash	$1,000,000
20-year 14% mortgage	5,000,000
	$6,000,000

2. Monthly debt service on the mortgage is $62,175.
3. Depreciation is calculated using the straight-line method over a 40-year life.
4. The plant has a 50,000-unit capacity. It is expected that the market will absorb 3,500 new units in the first 6 months of operation and 7,000 new units per year thereafter.
5. The new factory will require 15 new employees to begin operations and 3 new employees each year as production increases.
6. Excess cash is first used to pay down the revolving credit line. Any additional excess is invested in certificates of deposit at prime less 1.
7. Prime rates are as follows:

Jan.–June	19X1	17%	Jan.–Dec.	19X2	14%
July–Sept.	19X1	16%	Jan.–June	19X3	14%
Oct.–Dec.	19X1	14%	July–Dec.	19X3	13%

Example 9-1.
MBL Mfg. Co. Cash Flow Forecast: Final Format I

MBL Manufacturing Company
Forecasted Cash Flow for the Three Years Ending 12/31

	19X1	19X2	19X3
Receipts:			
Accounts Receivable and Cash Sales	$3,806,139	$4,177,259	$5,047,454
Service Contracts	306,416	330,000	342,618
Investments	711,094	528,775	588,800
Borrowings	260,215	—	—
Total Receipts	5,083,864	5,036,034	5,978,872
Disbursements:			
Salaries and Benefits	840,902	1,029,267	1,205,149
Purchases of Inventory	438,057	1,219,584	1,420,320
Debt Payments	559,045	1,172,179	1,292,538
Repairs and Maintenance	41,345	48,780	52,817
Accounting	32,000	34,000	37,000
Utilities	15,091	20,111	25,858
Lease Payments	2,213	2,213	2,213
Tax Payments	626,202	766,368	1,152,449
Purchase of Building	1,000,000	—	—
Other	60,800	62,000	68,000
Total Disbursements	3,615,655	4,354,502	5,256,344
Total Cash Flow	$1,468,209	$ 681,532	$ 722,528

Example 9-2.
MBL Mfg. Co. Cash Flow Forecast: Final Format II

MBL Manufacturing Company
Forecasted Cash Flow For the Three Years Ending 12/31

	19X1	19X2	19X3
Operating Receipts:			
Accounts Receivable and Cash Sales	$ 3,441,101	$3,246,040	$ 3,464,381
Service Contracts	306,416	330,000	342,618
Investments	322,839	284,650	290,432
Total Operating Receipts	4,070,356	3,860,690	4,097,431
Operating Disbursements:			
Salaries and Benefits	763,009	846,832	987,481
Purchasing of Inventory	351,785	952,830	937,800
Interest Payments	73,995	52,864	46,438
Repairs and Maintenance	41,345	48,780	52,817
Accounting	32,000	34,000	37,000
Mortgage Payments	12,000	13,000	—
Utilities	11,716	12,486	16,483
Lease Payments	2,213	2,213	2,213
Tax Payments	683,381	724,861	847,932
Other	60,800	62,000	68,000
Total Operating Disbursements	2,032,244	2,749,866	2,996,164
Net Operating Cash Flow	2,038,112	1,110,824	1,101,267
Nonoperating:			
Bond Maturities	300,000	—	—
Factoring Proceeds (payments)	260,215	(260,215)	—
Debt Maturities	(100,000)	(100,000)	(500,000)
Total Excess (Deficit)	2,498,327	750,609	601,267
Effect of Purchasing New Facility:			
Increased Sales	365,038	931,219	1,583,073
Down Payment	(1,000,000)	—	—
Debt Payments	(373,050)	(746,100)	(746,100)
Increased Expenses	(110,361)	(498,321)	(1,014,080)
Interest earned on excess cash	88,255	244,125	298,368
	(1,030,118)	(69,077)	121,261
Total Revised Cash Flow	$ 1,468,209	$ 681,532	$ 722,528

Conclusion

Now that we have gone through the entire forecasting process you can see
the importance of cash flow in the ongoing business operations of a company. Remember that cash flow forecasts are management tools. They
should be tailored to meet management's needs and they should be
designed to be sensitive to changing assumptions. If these goals can be
attained, cash flow forecasts can become one of the most useful planning
tools available to management.

Exhibit 9-1
MBL Mfg. Co.
Forecasting Worksheet Assuming Purchase of New Facility
Cash Flow for 19X1

	Receipts				Disbursements										Excess (Deficit) Cash
	Sales	Service Contracts	Investments	Borrowings	Salaries and Benefits	Inventory Purchases	Debt Payments	Repairs and Maintenance	Accounting	Utilities	Lease Payments	Tax Payments	Other	Down Payment on Factory	
Balance per "as is" cash flow	$3,441,101	$306,416	$622,839	$260,215	$763,009	$351,785	$185,995	$41,345	$32,000	$11,716	$2,213	$683,381	$60,800		
Down payment on factory														$1,000,000	
Debt service on mfg.							373,050								
Heat, light, and power										3,375					
Wages and benefits:															
Salaries					73,394										
FICA					4,499										
Sales	365,038														
Inventory purchases						86,272									
Tax payments												(97,776)			
	3,806,139	306,416	622,839	260,215	840,902	438,057	559,045	41,345	32,000	15,091	2,213	585,605	60,800	1,000,000	$1,420,551
Interest on excess cash			88,255									40,597			47,658
	$3,806,139	$306,416	$711,094	$260,215	$840,902	$438,057	$559,045	$41,345	$32,000	$15,091	$2,213	$626,202	$60,800	$1,000,000	$1,468,209

Exhibit 9-2
MBL Mfg. Co.
Forecasting Worksheet Assuming Purchase of New Facility
Cash Flow for 19X2

	Receipts				Disbursements									Excess (Deficit) Cash
	Sales	Service Contracts	Investments	Borrowings	Salaries and Benefits	Inventory Purchases	Debt Payments	Repairs and Maintenance	Accounting	Utilities	Lease Payments	Tax Payments	Other	
Balance per "as is" cash flow	$3,246,040	$330,00	$284,650		$ 846,832	$ 952,830	$ 426,079	$48,780	$34,000	$12,486	$2,213	$724,861	$62,000	
Debt service on mortgage							746,100							
Heat, light and power										7,625				
Wages and benefits:														
Salaries					171,060									
FICA					11,375									
Sales	931,219													
Inventory purchases						266,754								
Tax payments												(70,790)		
	4,177,259	330,000	284,650	—	1,029,267	1,219,584	1,172,179	48,780	34,000	20,111	2,213	654,071	62,000	$549,704
Interest on excess cash			244,125									112,297		131,828
	$4,177,259	$330,000	$528,775		$1,029,267	$1,219,584	$1,172,179	$48,780	$34,000	$20,111	$2,213	$766,368	$62,000	$681,532

EXHIBIT 9-3

MBL Mfg. Co.

Forecasting Worksheet Assuming Purchase of New Facility

Cash Flow for 19X3

	Receipts				Disbursements									Excess (Deficit) Cash
	Sales	Service Contracts	Investments	Borrowings	Salaries and Benefits	Inventory Purchases	Debt Payments	Repairs and Maintenance	Accounting	Utilities	Lease Payments	Tax Payments	Other	
Balance per "as is" cash flow	$3,464,381	$342,618	$290,432		$987,481	$937,800	$546,438	$52,817	$37,000	$16,483	$2,213	$847,932	$68,000	
Debt payment on mortgage							746,100							
Heat, light, and power										9,375				
Wages and Benefits:														
Salaries					204,000									
FICA					13,668									
Sales	1,583,073													
Inventory purchases						482,520								
Tax payments												167,268		
	5,047,454	342,618	290,432		1,205,149	1,420,320	1,292,538	52,817	37,000	25,858	2,213	1,015,200	68,000	$561,409
Interest on excess cash			298,368									137,249		161,119
	$5,047,454	$342,618	$588,800		$1,205,149	$1,420,320	$1,292,538	$52,817	$37,000	$25,858	$2,213	$1,152,449	$68,000	$722,528

Compound Financial Tables

Throughout this text, we have referred to compound financial tables and have used them to simplify many of the cash flow calculations. In this section we will review the nature and use of these tables.[1] The basic concept behind compound financial tables is that money, if invested, will earn more money. Therefore, if we had a choice of getting a sum of money today versus an equal sum of money at some future time, we would always accept the money today. However, if we were able to invest a lower sum of money in a bank (or some other investment) and earn interest such that at maturity we would have an amount of money exactly equal to what was then due us, we would be indifferent as to which of the two alternatives we would accept. Thus, once we have determined the rate of return with which we are satisfied, we can always determine what a given sum of money is "worth" at any given point of time.

Basically, there are two ways of valuing money:

1. *Present value.* This is what money due in the future is worth today.
2. *Future value.* This is what money invested today at a specific rate of interest will be worth in the future.

Both present value and future value are functions of time and the frequency of interest compounding.

---

[1]The compound financial tables included at the end of this appendix (Exhibits A-1 through A-8) have been reproduced from publication No. 376, *Financial Compound Interest and Annuity Tables*, 5th ed., copyright 1978, pp. 386–387, 558–559, 670–671, and 730–731, Financial Publishing Company, Boston, Mass.

161

Compound Interest

Interest or "money earned" is usually compounded in one of four ways:

1. *Annually.* This method assumes that interest is earned once a year. Thus, $100 at 10%* would earn $10.00 in one year.

$$\$100 \times 10\% \times 1 = \$10$$

2. *Semiannually.* This method assumes that interest is earned twice a year. Thus, $100 at 10%* would earn $10.25 in one year.

$100.00 × 10% × 1/2 =	$ 5.00
105.00 × 10% × 1/2 =	5.25
	$10.25

3. *Quarterly.* This method assumes that interest is earned four times a year. Thus, $100 at 10%* would earn $10.38 in one year.

$100.00 × 10% × 1/4 =	$ 2.50
102.50 × 10% × 1/4 =	2.56
105.06 × 10% × 1/4 =	2.63
107.69 × 10% × 1/4 =	2.69
	$10.38

4. *Monthly.* This method assumes that interest is earned 12 times a year. Thus, $100 at 10%* would earn $10.47 in one year.

$100.00 × 10% × 1/12 =	$ 0.83
100.83 × 10% × 1/12 =	0.84
101.67 × 10% × 1/12 =	0.85
102.52 × 10% × 1/12 =	0.85
103.37 × 10% × 1/12 =	0.86
104.23 × 10% × 1/12 =	0.87
105.10 × 10% × 1/12 =	0.88
105.98 × 10% × 1/12 =	0.88
106.86 × 10% × 1/12 =	0.89
107.75 × 10% × 1/12 =	0.90
108.65 × 10% × 1/12 =	0.91
109.56 × 10% × 1/12 =	0.91
	$10.47

*For illustrative purposes, a 10% interest rate will be used as the earning rate of money throughout this appendix.

Compound Financial Tables

A standard book of compound financial tables typically contains rates ranging from 1% to 300%. Usually, those interest rates that are close to the market rate of interest at the date the tables are published are broken down into ⅛% intervals. Each table can be used to compute interest monthly, quarterly, semiannually, or annually. Thus, the periods indicated in the tables can represent months, quarters, semiannual periods, or years.

For example, Exhibit A-1 can be read as follows:

- If the periods are months, it is a 10% table.
- If the periods are quarters, it is a 3⅓% table.
- If the periods are six-month intervals, it is a 1⅔% table.
- If the periods are years, it is a ⅚% table.

There are six basic compound financial tables, each based on different assumptions as to the timing of money paid. As we have previously seen, these tables can be applied to areas like sales and inventory, as well as money and money market instruments. By understanding the concept and mathematics of each table, it is easy to adapt a given table to your forecasting needs.

AMOUNT OF 1

This table can be used to calculate how money will grow if it is allowed to compound interest periodically, like a savings deposit or a CD with compounding. We previously calculated the annual interest earned on $100 compounded for various periods. These detailed calculations can be significantly simplified by using the amount of 1 table as follows:

	Periods			
	Monthly	**Quarterly**	**Semiannually**	**Annually**
Original investment	$100.00	$100.00	$100.00	$100.00
Amount of 1 factor*	1.1047	1.1038	1.1025	1.100
	$110.47	$100.38	$110.25	$110.00

*See Exhibits A-1, A-3, A-5, and A-7 for factors to be used.

Note that for the monthly calculation, we used the "amount of 1" for the twelth period; for the quarterly calculation we used it for the fourth period; for the semiannual calculation we used it for the second period; and for the annual calculation we used it for the first period, from the appropriate table. The greater the time period to be forecasted, the easier the table makes our calculation. For example, if we wanted to calculate by hand the amount $100 would earn at 10% for three years and four months, we would be required to perform 40 separate calculations. By using the table we would merely replace the 1.1047 with 1.3937 and obtain the answer.

AMOUNT OF 1 PER PERIOD

This table can be used to compute how money deposited periodically will grow if it is allowed to compound interest each period. If we want to forecast how much we will have at the end of six months if we invest $100 at the end of each period (for example, each month, each quarter, each six months) in a savings account or CD, the following calculations could be made:

	Periods			
	Monthly	**Quarterly**	**Semiannually**	**Annually**
Amount per period	$100.00	$100.00	$100.00	$100.00
Amount of 1 per period factor*	6.1264	2.0250	1.000	—
	$612.64	$202.50	$100.00	—

*See Exhibits A-1, A-3, A-5, and A-7 for factors to be used.

Note that if deposits were made monthly, there would be six deposits plus interest for five months since no interest would be paid on the last deposit which was made at the end of the period. Similarly, if the deposits were made quarterly, there would be two deposits made in a six-month period, with only one deposit earning interest. If the deposits were made semiannually, there would only be one deposit made at the end of the period and no interest would be earned because the deposit was made at the end of our six-month forecast period.

Let's assume we wanted to deposit our $100 at the beginning of each period rather than at the end of the period. This calculation can be done by simply modifying our use of the table. Now, we would use the factor for one additional period and then subtract 1. Thus, the preceding problem would be solved as follows:

	Compounding			
	Monthly	Quarterly	Semiannually	Annually
Amount per period	$100.00	$100.00	$100.00	$100.00
Amount of 1 per period factor:*				
7.1775 − 1.000	6.1775			
3.0756 − 1.000		2.0756		
2.0500 − 1.000			1.0500	—
	$617.75	$207.56	$105.00	$100.00

*See Exhibits A-1, A-3, A-5, and A-7 for factors to be used.

Note that although the same number of deposits are made, more interest is earned by depositing at the beginning of a period, since the money begins to earn interest from the first full period.

SINKING FUND

This table can be used to compute the amount required to be deposited periodically in order to obtain a specified amount in the future. For example, how much money must be retained and invested at the *end* of each period at 10% in order to meet a debt obligation, purchase new equipment, etc.? Let's assume we need $3,500 in 24 months in order to purchase a machine. The periodic payments would be calculated as follows:

	Periods			
	Monthly	Quarterly	Semiannually	Annually
Amount needed in future	$3,500	$3,500	$3,500	$3,500
Sinking fund factor*	.0378	.1145	.2320	.4762
	$132.30	$400.75	$812.00	$1,666.70

*See Exhibits A-1, A-3, A-5, and A-7 for factors to be used.

To understand the concept behind the table, let's examine more closely the semiannual calculation. This calculation basically tells us that if we put $812.00 aside every three months earning 10%, we will have $3,500 at the end of two years. If this calculation were to be done manually it would be calculated as follows:

$812.00 × 10% × $\frac{3}{12}$ = $40.60
$812.00 + 812.00 + 40.60 × 10% × $\frac{3}{12}$ = $83.23
$812.00 + 812.00 + 812.00 + 40.60 + 83.23 × 10% × $\frac{3}{12}$ = $127.99
$812.00 + 812.00 + 812.00 + 812.00 + 40.60 + 83.23 + 127.99 = $3,500.00*

*Total is rounded.

PRESENT WORTH OF 1

This table can be used to calculate what an amount of money due in the future is worth today. It can determine how much of a discount you should give to entice a customer to prepay, assuming you could invest the proceeds in an account earning 10% compounded, monthly, quarterly, semiannually, or annually. If an account receivable due in 360 days totaled $4,322, the following calculation would be made:

	Periods			
	Monthly	Quarterly	Semiannually	Annually
Amount due in the future	$4,322	$4,322	4,322	$4,322
Present worth of 1 factor*	.9052	.9060	.9070	.9091
	$3,912	$3,915	$3,920	$3,929

*See Exhibits A-2, A-4, A-6, and A-8 for factors to be used.

Thus, if you could earn 10% compounded monthly you would be willing to accept $3,912 today in full settlement of the $4,322 receivable. This type of analysis is especially useful in cash flow management in determining alternate sources of funds. If you are paying in excess of 10% on bank debt, it would be beneficial to offer the customer with the $4,322 receivable a $410 discount ($4,322 − $3,912) to prepay his or her account in order to use those funds to pay off the bank debt.

PRESENT WORTH OF 1 PER PERIOD

This table can be used to compute what money payable periodically is worth today. It can be used to determine how much of a discount you should give to entice a mortgagee to prepay. If an individual has 36 remaining monthly payments on a $35,000 mortgage with a constant payment of $900 per month and would be willing to prepay at a 10% discount rate, the cash to be received could be calculated as follows:

	Periods			
	Monthly	Quarterly	Semiannually	Annually
Payment per period	$ 900	$900 × 3	$900 × 6	$900 × 12
Present worth of 1 per period factor*	30.9912	10.2578	5.0757	2.4869
	$27,892	$27,696	$27,409	$26,859

*See Exhibits A-2, A-4, A-6, and A-8 for factors to be used.

Thus, if the $900 were a monthly payment the individual would be willing to prepay the obligation for $27,892.

PARTIAL PAYMENT

This table can be used to determine the periodic payments required to pay off a loan (for example, a mortgage or a note on property, plant, and equipment). If we wish to borrow $100,000 for five years, the periodic payments would be calculated as follows:

	Periods			
	Monthly	**Quarterly**	**Semiannually**	**Annually**
Amount borrowed (loaned)	$100,000	$100,000	$100,000	$100,000
Partial payment factor*	.0212	.0641	.1295	.2638
	$ 2,120	$ 6,410	$ 12,950	$ 26,380

*See Exhibits A-2, A-4, A-6, and A-8 for factors to be used.

The previous six tables used alone or in combination can be used to solve many different mathematical problems in our forecast process. For example, in Chapter 3 we were able to evaluate a bond at some point in the future by applying the tables to various streams of cash flow. In this case, we used:

1. The present worth of $1 per period table for interest on the bond.
2. The present worth of $1 table for the principal payment at maturity.

Keep in mind that these tables deal in "periods" and a period can be any amount of time. If we are working with a problem that deals with a one-year time period, then we must be careful when using the quarterly table to use the factor for four periods.

Another important point to remember when using compound financial tables is that although these tables were designed for money calculations, they also can be used for other nonmonetary applications. For example:

Projected growth rate for sales
Projected rate of inventory buildup

Other Methods of Computing Money Values

Although this appendix deals with compound financial tables, it would be unfair to give the impression that they are the only way to compute values. There are several other methods available.

1. *In-house or time-sharing computers.* Most computer systems have software available that will calculate financial information (i.e., present value, future value, internal rates of return, payback periods, etc.). In addition, almost all of the hand calculations and worksheet compilations we have prepared can easily be done by computer. Several software vendors have inexpensive "canned" forecasting programs available.

2. *Pocket calculators.* Most calculator companies currently sell hand-held calculators which are capable of doing chain calculations such as depreciation, future value, present value, etc. Several of these calculators are sold for under $100.

3. *Financial publishing tables.* There are several financial publishing companies who will prepare, for a nominal fee, mortgage amortization tables, depreciation schedules, etc., based on any assumptions provided to them.

Compound
Financial
Tables

RATE 5/6%	P E R I O D S	AMOUNT OF 1 How $1 left at compound interest will grow.	AMOUNT OF 1 PER PERIOD How $1 deposited periodically will grow.	SINKING FUND Periodic deposit that will grow to $1 at future date.
.00833333 per period	1	1.008 333 3333	1.000 000 0000	1.000 000 0000
	2	1.016 736 1111	2.008 333 3333	.497 925 3112
	3	1.025 208 9120	3.025 069 4444	.330 570 9235
	4	1.033 752 3196	4.050 278 3565	.246 896 6110
	5	1.042 366 9223	5.084 030 6761	.196 694 3285
	6	1.051 053 3133	6.126 397 5984	.163 228 0609
	7	1.059 812 0909	7.177 450 9117	.139 325 2301
	8	1.068 643 8584	8.237 263 0027	.121 399 5474
	9	1.077 549 2238	9.305 906 8610	.107 458 0298
	10	1.086 528 8007	10.383 456 0849	.096 307 0477
	11	1.095 583 2074	11.469 984 8856	.087 184 0730
	12	1.104 713 0674	12.565 568 0930	.079 582 5539
	13	1.113 919 0097	13.670 281 1604	.073 151 3850
	14	1.123 201 6681	14.784 200 1701	.067 639 7768
	15	1.132 561 6820	15.907 401 8382	.062 863 8171
	16	1.141 999 6960	17.039 963 5201	.058 685 5716
	17	1.151 516 3601	18.181 963 2161	.054 999 5613
	18	1.161 112 3298	19.333 479 5763	.051 723 7467
	19	1.170 788 2659	20.494 591 9061	.048 793 3600
	20	1.180 544 8348	21.665 380 1720	.046 156 5868
ANNUALLY If compounded *annually* nominal annual rate is 5/6%	21	1.190 382 7084	22.845 925 0067	.043 771 4822
	22	1.200 302 5643	24.036 307 7151	.041 603 7277
	23	1.210 305 0857	25.236 610 2794	.039 624 9730
	24	1.220 390 9614	26.446 915 3651	.037 811 5930
	25	1.230 560 8861	27.667 306 3264	.036 143 7427
	26	1.240 815 5601	28.897 867 2125	.034 604 6299
	27	1.251 155 6898	30.138 682 7726	.033 179 9504
	28	1.261 581 9872	31.389 838 4624	.031 857 4433
	29	1.272 095 1704	32.651 420 4496	.030 626 5389
	30	1.282 695 9635	33.923 515 6200	.029 478 0768
SEMIANNUALLY If compounded *semiannually* nominal annual rate is 1 2/3%	31	1.293 385 0965	35.206 211 5835	.028 404 0786
	32	1.304 163 3057	36.499 596 6800	.027 397 5630
	33	1.315 031 3332	37.803 759 9857	.026 452 3952
	34	1.325 989 9277	39.118 791 3189	.025 563 1620
	35	1.337 039 8437	40.444 781 2465	.024 725 0688
	36	1.348 181 8424	41.781 821 0903	.023 933 8539
	37	1.359 416 6911	43.130 002 9327	.023 185 7160
	38	1.370 745 1635	44.489 419 6238	.022 477 2543
	39	1.382 168 0399	45.860 164 7873	.021 805 4166
	40	1.393 686 1069	47.242 332 8272	.021 167 4560
QUARTERLY If compounded *quarterly* nominal annual rate is 3 1/3%	41	1.405 300 1578	48.636 018 9341	.020 560 8934
	42	1.417 010 9924	50.041 319 0919	.019 983 4860
	43	1.428 819 4174	51.458 330 0843	.019 433 1996
	44	1.440 726 2458	52.887 149 5017	.018 908 1849
	45	1.452 732 2979	54.327 875 7475	.018 406 7569
	46	1.464 838 4004	55.780 608 0454	.017 927 3772
	47	1.477 045 3870	57.245 446 4458	.017 468 6383
	48	1.489 354 0986	58.722 491 8329	.017 029 2501
	49	1.501 765 3828	60.211 845 9315	.016 608 0276
	50	1.514 280 0943	61.713 611 3142	.016 203 8808
MONTHLY If compounded *monthly* nominal annual rate is .10%	51	1.526 899 0951	63.227 891 4085	.015 815 8050
	52	1.539 623 2542	64.754 790 5036	.015 442 8729
	53	1.552 453 4480	66.294 413 7578	.015 084 2272
	54	1.565 390 5600	67.846 867 2058	.014 739 0741
	55	1.578 435 4814	69.412 257 7658	.014 406 6773
	56	1.591 589 1104	70.990 693 2472	.014 086 3535
	57	1.604 852 3530	72.582 282 3576	.013 777 4670
	58	1.618 226 1226	74.187 134 7106	.013 479 4261
	59	1.631 711 3403	75.805 360 8332	.013 191 6792
	60	1.645 308 9348	77.437 072 1734	.012 913 7114
$i = .00833333$ $j_{(2)} = .01666666$ $j_{(4)} = .03333333$ $j_{(12)} = .1$	**n**	$s=(1+i)^n$	$s_{\overline{n}|}=\dfrac{(1+i)^n-1}{i}$	$\dfrac{1}{s_{\overline{n}|}}=\dfrac{i}{(1+i)^n-1}$

PRESENT WORTH OF 1 — What $1 due in the future is worth today.	PRESENT WORTH OF 1 PER PERIOD — What $1 payable periodically is worth today.	PARTIAL PAYMENT — Annuity worth $1 today. Periodic payment necessary to pay off a loan of $1.	PERIODS	RATE 5/6%
.991 735 5372	.991 735 5372	1.008 333 3333	1	
.983 539 3757	1.975 274 9129	.506 258 6445	2	
.975 410 9511	2.950 685 8640	.338 904 2569	3	.00833333
.967 349 7036	3.918 035 5677	.255 229 9444	4	per period
.959 355 0780	4.877 390 6456	.205 027 6619	5	
.951 426 5236	5.828 817 1692	.171 561 3942	6	
.943 563 4945	6.772 380 6637	.147 658 5635	7	
.935 765 4491	7.708 146 1127	.129 732 8807	8	
.928 031 8503	8.636 177 9630	.115 791 9631	9	
.920 362 1656	9.556 540 1286	.104 640 3810	10	
.912 755 8667	10.469 295 9953	.095 517 4064	11	
.905 212 4298	11.374 508 4251	.087 915 8872	12	
.897 731 3353	12.272 239 7605	.081 484 7183	13	
.890 312 0681	13.162 551 8285	.075 973 1102	14	
.882 954 1171	14.045 505 9457	.071 197 1505	15	
.875 656 9757	14.921 162 9213	.067 018 9050	16	
.868 420 1411	15.789 583 0625	.063 332 8946	17	
.861 243 1152	16.650 826 1777	.060 057 0800	18	
.854 125 4035	17.504 951 5811	.057 126 6933	19	
.847 066 5159	18.352 018 0970	.054 489 9201	20	
.840 065 9661	19.192 084 0631	.052 104 8155	21	ANNUALLY
.833 123 2722	20.025 207 3354	.049 937 0610	22	If compounded annually
.826 237 9559	20.851 445 2913	.047 958 3063	23	nominal annual rate is
.819 409 5430	21.670 854 8343	.046 144 9263	24	
.812 637 5634	22.483 492 3977	.044 477 0760	25	5/6%
.805 921 5504	23.289 413 9481	.042 937 9632	26	
.799 261 0418	24.088 674 9898	.041 513 2837	27	
.792 655 5786	24.881 330 5684	.040 190 7767	28	
.786 104 7060	25.667 435 2745	.038 959 8723	29	
.779 607 9729	26.447 043 2474	.037 811 4102	30	
.773 164 9318	27.220 208 1793	.036 737 4119	31	SEMIANNUALLY
.766 775 1390	27.986 983 3183	.035 730 8963	32	If compounded semiannually
.760 438 1544	28.747 421 4727	.034 785 7286	33	nominal annual rate is
.754 153 5415	29.501 575 0142	.033 896 4953	34	
.747 920 8677	30.249 495 8819	.033 058 4022	35	1⅔%
.741 739 7035	30.991 235 5853	.032 267 1872	36	
.735 609 6233	31.726 845 2086	.031 519 0494	37	
.729 530 2049	32.456 375 4135	.030 810 5877	38	
.723 501 0296	33.179 876 4431	.030 138 7500	39	
.717 521 6823	33.897 398 1254	.029 500 7893	40	
.711 591 7510	34.608 989 8764	.028 894 2267	41	QUARTERLY
.705 710 8275	35.314 700 7039	.028 316 8193	42	If compounded quarterly
.699 878 5066	36.014 579 2105	.027 766 5329	43	nominal annual rate is
.694 094 3867	36.708 673 5972	.027 241 5182	44	
.688 358 0694	37.397 031 6666	.026 740 0902	45	3⅓%
.682 669 1598	38.079 700 8264	.026 260 7105	46	
.677 027 2659	38.756 728 0923	.025 801 9717	47	
.671 431 9992	39.428 160 0915	.025 362 5834	48	
.665 882 9745	40.094 043 0660	.024 941 3609	49	
.660 379 8094	40.754 422 8754	.024 537 2141	50	MONTHLY
.654 922 1250	41.409 345 0003	.024 149 1383	51	If compounded monthly
.649 509 5455	42.058 854 5458	.023 776 2062	52	nominal annual rate is
.644 141 6980	42.702 996 2438	.023 417 5605	53	
.638 818 2129	43.341 814 4566	.023 072 4074	54	
.633 538 7235	43.975 353 1801	.022 740 0107	55	10%
.628 302 8663	44.603 656 0464	.022 419 6868	56	
.623 110 2806	45.226 766 3270	.022 110 8003	57	
.617 960 6089	45.844 726 9359	.021 812 7594	58	i = .00833333
.612 853 4964	46.457 580 4323	.021 525 0125	59	j(2) = .01666666
.607 788 5915	47.065 369 0238	.021 247 0447	60	j(4) = .03333333
$v^n = \dfrac{1}{(1+i)^n}$	$a_{\overline{n}|} = \dfrac{1-v^n}{i}$	$\dfrac{1}{a_{\overline{n}|}} = \dfrac{i}{1-v^n}$	n	j(12) = .1

RATE **2½%**	P E R I O D S	AMOUNT OF 1 *How $1 left at compound interest will grow.*	AMOUNT OF 1 PER PERIOD *How $1 deposited periodically will grow.*	SINKING FUND *Periodic deposit that will grow to $1 at future date.*
.025 *per period*	1	1.025 000 0000	1.000 000 0000	1.000 000 0000
	2	1.050 625 0000	2.025 000 0000	.493 827 1605
	3	1.076 890 6250	3.075 625 0000	.325 137 1672
	4	1.103 812 8906	4.152 515 6250	.240 817 8777
	5	1.131 408 2129	5.256 328 5156	.190 246 8609
	6	1.159 693 4182	6.387 736 7285	.156 549 9711
	7	1.188 685 7537	7.547 430 1467	.132 495 4296
	8	1.218 402 8975	8.736 115 9004	.114 467 3458
	9	1.248 862 9699	9.954 518 7979	.100 456 8900
	10	1.280 084 5442	11.203 381 7679	.089 258 7632
	11	1.312 086 6578	12.483 466 3121	.080 105 9558
	12	1.344 888 8242	13.795 552 9699	.072 487 1270
	13	1.378 511 0449	15.140 441 7941	.066 048 2708
	14	1.412 973 8210	16.518 952 8390	.060 536 5249
	15	1.448 298 1665	17.931 926 6599	.055 766 4561
	16	1.484 505 6207	19.380 224 8264	.051 598 9886
	17	1.521 618 2612	20.864 730 4471	.047 927 7699
	18	1.559 658 7177	22.386 348 7083	.044 670 0805
	19	1.598 650 1856	23.946 007 4260	.041 760 6151
	20	1.638 616 4403	25.544 657 6116	.039 147 1287
ANNUALLY If compounded *annually* nominal annual rate is **2½%**	21	1.679 581 8513	27.183 274 0519	.036 787 3273
	22	1.721 571 3976	28.862 855 9032	.034 646 6061
	23	1.764 610 6825	30.584 427 3008	.032 696 3781
	24	1.808 725 9496	32.349 037 9833	.030 912 8204
	25	1.853 944 0983	34.157 763 9329	.029 275 9210
	26	1.900 292 7008	36.011 708 0312	.027 768 7467
	27	1.947 800 0183	37.912 000 7320	.026 376 8722
	28	1.996 495 0188	39.859 800 7503	.025 087 9327
	29	2.046 407 3942	41.856 295 7690	.023 891 2685
	30	2.097 567 5791	43.902 703 1633	.022 777 6407
SEMIANNUALLY If compounded *semiannually* nominal annual rate is **5%**	31	2.150 006 7686	46.000 270 7424	.021 739 0025
	32	2.203 756 9378	48.150 277 5109	.020 768 3123
	33	2.258 850 8612	50.354 034 4487	.019 859 3819
	34	2.315 322 1327	52.612 885 3099	.019 006 7508
	35	2.373 205 1861	54.928 207 4426	.018 205 5823
	36	2.432 535 3157	57.301 412 6287	.017 451 5767
	37	2.493 348 6986	59.733 947 9444	.016 740 8992
	38	2.555 682 4161	62.227 296 6430	.016 070 1180
	39	2.619 574 4765	64.782 979 0591	.015 436 1534
	40	2.685 063 8384	67.402 553 5356	.014 836 2332
QUARTERLY If compounded *quarterly* nominal annual rate is **10%**	41	2.752 190 4343	70.087 617 3740	.014 267 8555
	42	2.820 995 1952	72.839 807 8083	.013 728 7567
	43	2.891 520 0751	75.660 803 0035	.013 216 8833
	44	2.963 808 0770	78.552 323 0786	.012 730 3683
	45	3.037 903 2789	81.516 131 1556	.012 267 5106
	46	3.113 850 8609	84.554 034 4345	.011 826 7568
	47	3.191 697 1324	87.667 885 2954	.011 406 6855
	48	3.271 489 5607	90.859 582 4277	.011 005 9938
	49	3.353 276 7997	94.131 071 9884	.010 623 4847
	50	3.437 108 7197	97.484 348 7881	.010 258 0569
MONTHLY If compounded *monthly* nominal annual rate is **30%**	51	3.523 036 4377	100.921 457 5078	.009 908 6956
	52	3.611 112 3486	104.444 493 9455	.009 574 4635
	53	3.701 390 1574	108.055 606 2942	.009 254 4944
	54	3.793 924 9113	111.756 996 4515	.008 947 9856
	55	3.888 773 0341	115.550 921 3628	.008 654 1932
$i = .025$ $j_{(2)} = .05$ $j_{(4)} = .1$ $j_{(12)} = .3$	56	3.985 992 3599	119.439 694 3969	.008 372 4260
	57	4.085 642 1689	123.425 686 7568	.008 102 0412
	58	4.187 783 2231	127.511 328 9257	.007 842 4404
	59	4.292 477 8037	131.699 112 1489	.007 593 0656
	60	4.399 789 7488	135.991 589 9526	.007 353 3959
	n	$s=(1+i)^n$	$s_{\overline{n}|}=\dfrac{(1+i)^n-1}{i}$	$\dfrac{1}{s_{\overline{n}|}}=\dfrac{i}{(1+i)^n-1}$

PRESENT WORTH OF 1 *What $1 due in the future is worth today.*	PRESENT WORTH OF 1 PER PERIOD *What $1 payable periodically is worth today.*	PARTIAL PAYMENT *Annuity worth $1 today.* *Periodic payment necessary to pay off a loan of $1.*	PERIODS	RATE 2½%
.975 609 7561	.975 609 7561	1.025 000 0000	1	
.951 814 3962	1.927 424 1523	.518 827 1605	2	
.928 599 4109	2.856 023 5632	.350 137 1672	3	.025
.905 950 6448	3.761 974 2080	.265 817 8777	4	*per period*
.883 854 2876	4.645 828 4956	.215 246 8609	5	
.862 296 8660	5.508 125 3616	.181 549 9711	6	
.841 265 2351	6.349 390 5967	.157 495 4296	7	
.820 746 5708	7.170 137 1675	.139 467 3458	8	
.800 728 3618	7.970 865 5292	.125 456 8900	9	
.781 198 4017	8.752 063 9310	.114 258 7632	10	
.762 144 7822	9.514 208 7131	.105 105 9558	11	
.743 555 8850	10.257 764 5982	.097 487 1270	12	
.725 420 3757	10.983 184 9738	.091 048 2708	13	
.707 727 1958	11.690 912 1696	.085 536 5249	14	
.690 465 5568	12.381 377 7264	.080 766 4561	15	
.673 624 9335	13.055 002 6599	.076 598 9886	16	
.657 195 0571	13.712 197 7170	.072 927 7699	17	
.641 165 9093	14.353 363 6264	.069 670 0805	18	
.625 527 7164	14.978 891 3428	.066 760 6151	19	
.610 270 9429	15.589 162 2856	.064 147 1287	20	
.595 386 2857	16.184 548 5714	.061 787 3273	21	ANNUALLY If compounded *annually* nominal annual rate is
.580 864 6690	16.765 413 2404	.059 646 6061	22	
.566 697 2380	17.332 110 4784	.057 696 3781	23	
.552 875 3542	17.884 985 8326	.055 912 8204	24	2½%
.539 390 5894	18.424 376 4220	.054 275 9210	25	
.526 234 7214	18.950 611 1434	.052 768 7467	26	
.513 399 7282	19.464 010 8717	.051 376 8722	27	
.500 877 7836	19.964 888 6553	.050 087 9327	28	
.488 661 2523	20.453 549 9076	.048 891 2685	29	
.476 742 6852	20.930 292 5928	.047 777 6407	30	SEMIANNUALLY If compounded *semiannually* nominal annual rate is
.465 114 8148	21.395 407 4076	.046 739 0025	31	
.453 770 5510	21.849 177 9586	.045 768 3123	32	
.442 702 9766	22.291 880 9352	.044 859 3819	33	
.431 905 3430	22.723 786 2783	.044 006 7508	34	5%
.421 371 0664	23.145 157 3447	.043 205 5823	35	
.411 093 7233	23.556 251 0680	.042 451 5767	36	
.401 067 0471	23.957 318 1151	.041 740 8992	37	
.391 284 9240	24.348 603 0391	.041 070 1180	38	
.381 741 3893	24.730 344 4284	.040 436 1534	39	
.372 430 6237	25.102 775 0521	.039 836 2332	40	QUARTERLY If compounded *quarterly* nominal annual rate is
.363 346 9499	25.466 122 0020	.039 267 8555	41	
.354 484 8292	25.820 606 8313	.038 728 7567	42	
.345 838 8578	26.166 445 6890	.038 216 8833	43	
.337 403 7637	26.503 849 4527	.037 730 3683	44	10%
.329 174 4036	26.833 023 8563	.037 267 5106	45	
.321 145 7596	27.154 169 6159	.036 826 7568	46	
.313 312 9362	27.467 482 5521	.036 406 6855	47	
.305 671 1573	27.773 153 7094	.036 005 9938	48	
.298 215 7632	28.071 369 4726	.035 623 4847	49	
.290 942 2080	28.362 311 6805	.035 258 0569	50	MONTHLY If compounded *monthly* nominal annual rate is
.283 846 0566	28.646 157 7371	.034 908 6956	51	
.276 922 9820	28.923 080 7191	.034 574 4635	52	
.270 168 7629	29.193 249 4821	.034 254 4944	53	
.263 579 2809	29.456 828 7630	.033 947 9856	54	30%
.257 150 5180	29.713 979 2810	.033 654 1932	55	
.250 878 5541	29.964 857 8351	.033 372 4260	56	
.244 759 5650	30.209 617 4001	.033 102 0412	57	
.238 789 8195	30.448 407 2196	.032 842 4404	58	$i = .025$
.232 965 6776	30.681 372 8972	.032 593 0656	59	$j^{(2)} = .05$
.227 283 5879	30.908 656 4851	.032 353 3959	60	$j^{(4)} = .1$
$v^n = \dfrac{1}{(1+i)^n}$	$a_{\overline{n}|} = \dfrac{1-v^n}{i}$	$\dfrac{1}{a_{\overline{n}|}} = \dfrac{i}{1-v^n}$	n	$j^{(12)} = .3$

RATE 5%	P E R I O D S	AMOUNT OF 1 *How $1 left at compound interest will grow.*	AMOUNT OF 1 PER PERIOD *How $1 deposited periodically will grow.*	SINKING FUND *Periodic deposit that will grow to $1 at future date.*
.05 *per period*	1 2 3 4 5	1.050 000 0000 1.102 500 0000 1.157 625 0000 1.215 506 2500 1.276 281 5625	1.000 000 0000 2.050 000 0000 3.152 500 0000 4.310 125 0000 5.525 631 2500	1.000 000 0000 .487 804 8780 .317 208 5646 .232 011 8326 .180 974 7981
	6 7 8 9 10	1.340 095 6406 1.407 100 4227 1.477 455 4438 1.551 328 2160 1.628 894 6268	6.801 912 8125 8.142 008 4531 9.549 108 8758 11.026 564 3196 12.577 892 5355	.147 017 4681 .122 819 8184 .104 721 8136 .090 690 0800 .079 504 5750
	11 12 13 14 15	1.710 339 3581 1.795 856 3260 1.885 649 1423 1.979 931 5994 2.078 928 1794	14.206 787 1623 15.917 126 5204 17.712 982 8465 19.598 631 9888 21.578 563 5882	.070 388 8915 .062 825 4100 .056 455 7652 .051 023 9695 .046 342 2876
	16 17 18 19 20	2.182 874 5884 2.292 018 3178 2.406 619 2337 2.526 950 1954 2.653 297 7051	23.657 491 7676 25.840 366 3560 28.132 384 6738 30.539 003 9075 33.065 954 1029	.042 269 9080 .038 699 1417 .035 546 2223 .032 745 0104 .030 242 5872
ANNUALLY If compounded *annually* nominal annual rate is 5%	21 22 23 24 25	2.785 962 5904 2.925 260 7199 3.071 523 7559 3.225 099 9437 3.386 354 9409	35.719 251 8080 38.505 214 3984 41.430 475 1184 44.501 998 8743 47.727 098 8180	.027 996 1071 .025 970 5086 .024 136 8219 .022 470 9008 .020 952 4573
	26 27 28 29 30	3.555 672 6879 3.733 456 3223 3.920 129 1385 4.116 135 5954 4.321 942 3752	51.113 453 7589 54.669 126 4468 58.402 582 7692 62.322 711 9076 66.438 847 5030	.019 564 3207 .018 291 8599 .017 122 5304 .016 045 5149 .015 051 4351
SEMIANNUALLY If compounded *semiannually* nominal annual rate is 10%	31 32 33 34 35	4.538 039 4939 4.764 941 4686 5.003 188 5420 5.253 347 9691 5.516 015 3676	70.760 789 8782 75.298 829 3721 80.063 770 8407 85.066 959 3827 90.320 307 3518	.014 132 1204 .013 280 4189 .012 490 0437 .011 755 4454 .011 071 7072
	36 37 38 39 40	5.791 816 1360 6.081 406 9428 6.385 477 2899 6.704 751 1544 7.039 988 7121	95.836 322 7194 101.628 138 8554 107.709 545 7982 114.095 023 0881 120.799 774 2425	.010 434 4571 .009 839 7945 .009 284 2282 .008 764 6242 .008 278 1612
QUARTERLY If compounded *quarterly* nominal annual rate is 20%	41 42 43 44 45	7.391 988 1477 7.761 587 5551 8.149 666 9329 8.557 150 2795 8.985 007 7935	127.839 762 9546 135.231 751 1023 142.993 338 6575 151.143 005 5903 159.700 155 8699	.007 822 2924 .007 394 7131 .006 993 3328 .006 616 2506 .006 261 7347
	46 47 48 49 50	9.434 258 1832 9.905 971 0923 10.401 269 6469 10.921 333 1293 11.467 399 7858	168.685 163 6633 178.119 421 8465 188.025 392 9388 198.426 662 5858 209.347 995 7151	.005 928 2036 .005 614 2109 .005 318 4306 .005 039 6453 .004 776 7355
MONTHLY If compounded *monthly* nominal annual rate is 60%	51 52 53 54 55	12.040 769 7750 12.642 808 2638 13.274 948 6770 13.938 696 1108 14.635 630 9164	220.815 395 5008 232.856 165 2759 245.498 973 5397 258.773 922 2166 272.712 618 3275	.004 528 6697 .004 294 4966 .004 073 3368 .003 864 3770 .003 666 8637
	56 57 58 59 60	15.367 412 4622 16.135 783 0853 16.942 572 2396 17.789 700 8515 18.679 185 8941	287.348 249 2439 302.715 661 7060 318.851 444 7913 335.794 017 0309 353.583 717 8825	.003 480 0978 .003 303 4300 .003 136 2568 .002 978 0161 .002 828 1845

$i = .05$
$j_{(2)} = .1$
$j_{(4)} = .2$
$j_{(12)} = .6$

n	$s = (1+i)^n$	$s_{\overline{n}\|} = \dfrac{(1+i)^n - 1}{i}$	$\dfrac{1}{s_{\overline{n}\|}} = \dfrac{i}{(1+i)^n - 1}$

PRESENT WORTH OF 1 — *What $1 due in the future is worth today.*	PRESENT WORTH OF 1 PER PERIOD — *What $1 payable periodically is worth today.*	PARTIAL PAYMENT — *Annuity worth $1 today. Periodic payment necessary to pay off a loan of $1.*	PERIODS	RATE — **5%**
.952 380 9524	.952 380 9524	1.050 000 0000	1	
.907 029 4785	1.859 410 4308	.537 804 8780	2	
.863 837 5985	2.723 248 0294	.367 208 5646	3	.05
.822 702 4748	3.545 950 5042	.282 011 8326	4	*per period*
.783 526 1665	4.329 476 6706	.230 974 7981	5	
.746 215 3966	5.075 692 0673	.197 017 4681	6	
.710 681 3301	5.786 373 3974	.172 819 8184	7	
.676 839 3620	6.463 212 7594	:154 721 8136	8	
.644 608 9162	7.107 821 6756	.140 690 0800	9	
.613 913 2535	7.721 734 9292	.129 504 5750	10	
.584 679 2891	8.306 414 2183	.120 388 8915	11	
.556 837 4182	8.863 251 6364	.112 825 4100	12	
.530 321 3506	9.393 572 9871	.106 455 7652	13	
.505 067 9530	9.898 640 9401	.101 023 9695	14	
.481 017 0981	10.379 658 0382	.096 342 2876	15	
.458 111 5220	10.837 769 5602	.092 269 9080	16	
.436 296 6876	11.274 066 2478	.088 699 1417	17	
.415 520 6549	11.689 586 9027	.085 546 2223	18	
.395 733 9570	12.085 320 8597	.082 745 0104	19	
.376 889 4829	12.462 210 3425	.080 242 5872	20	
.358 942 3646	12.821 152 7072	.077 996 1071	21	ANNUALLY — If compounded *annually* nominal annual rate is **5%**
.341 849 8711	13.163 002 5783	.075 970 5086	22	
.325 571 3058	13.488 573 8841	.074 136 8219	23	
.310 067 9103	13.798 641 7943	.072 470 9008	24	
.295 302 7717	14.093 944 5660	.070 952 4573	25	
.281 240 7350	14.375 185 3010	.069 564 3207	26	
.267 848 3190	14.643 033 6200	.068 291 8599	27	
.255 093 6371	14.898 127 2571	.067 122 5304	28	
.242 946 3211	15.141 073 5782	.066 045 5149	29	
.231 377 4487	15.372 451 0269	.065 051 4351	30	
.220 359 4749	15.592 810 5018	.064 132 1204	31	SEMIANNUALLY — If compounded *semiannually* nominal annual rate is **10%**
.209 866 1666	15.802 676 6684	.063 280 4189	32	
.199 872 5396	16.002 549 2080	.062 490 0437	33	
.190 354 7996	16.192 904 0076	.061 755 4454	34	
.181 290 2854	16.374 194 2929	.061 071 7072	35	
.172 657 4146	16.546 851 7076	.060 434 4571	36	
.164 435 6330	16.711 287 3405	.059 839 7945	37	
.156 605 3647	16.867 892 7053	.059 284 2282	38	
.149 147 9664	17.017 040 6717	.058 764 6242	39	
.142 045 6823	17.159 086 3540	.058 278 1612	40	QUARTERLY — If compounded *quarterly* nominal annual rate is **20%**
.135 281 6022	17.294 367 9562	.057 822 2924	41	
.128 839 6211	17.423 207 5773	.057 394 7131	42	
.122 704 4011	17.545 911 9784	.056 993 3328	43	
.116 861 3344	17.662 773 3128	.056 616 2506	44	
.111 296 5089	17.774 069 8217	.056 261 7347	45	
.105 996 6752	17.880 066 4968	.055 928 2036	46	
.100 949 2144	17.981 015 7113	.055 614 2109	47	
.096 142 1090	18.077 157 8203	.055 318 4306	48	
.091 563 9133	18.168 721 7336	.055 039 6453	49	
.087 203 7270	18.255 925 4606	.054 776 7355	50	MONTHLY — If compounded *monthly* nominal annual rate is **60%**
.083 051 1685	18.338 976 6291	.054 528 6697	51	
.079 096 3510	18.418 072 9801	.054 294 4966	52	
.075 329 8581	18.493 402 8382	.054 073 3368	53	
.071 742 7220	18.565 145 5602	.053 864 3770	54	
.068 326 4019	18.633 471 9621	.053 666 8637	55	
.065 072 7637	18.698 544 7258	.053 480 0978	56	
.061 974 0607	18.760 518 7865	.053 303 4300	57	$i = .05$
.059 022 9149	18.819 541 7014	.053 136 2568	58	$j_{(2)} = .1$
.056 212 2999	18.875 754 0013	.052 978 0161	59	$j_{(4)} = .2$
.053 535 5237	18.929 289 5251	.052 828 1845	60	$j_{(12)} = .6$
$v^n = \dfrac{1}{(1+i)^n}$	$a_{\overline{n}\rvert} = \dfrac{1-v^n}{i}$	$\dfrac{1}{a_{\overline{n}\rvert}} = \dfrac{i}{1-v^n}$	n	

175

RATE **10%**	P E R I O D S	AMOUNT OF 1 *How $1 left at compound interest will grow.*	AMOUNT OF 1 PER PERIOD *How $1 deposited periodically will grow.*	SINKING FUND *Periodic deposit that will grow to $1 at future date.*
.1 *per period*	1 2 3 4 5	1.100 000 0000 1.210 000 0000 1.331 000 0000 1.464 100 0000 1.610 510 0000	1.000 000 0000 2.100 000 0000 3.310 000 0000 4.641 000 0000 6.105 100 0000	1.000 000 0000 .476 190 4762 .302 114 8036 .215 470 8037 .163 797 4808
	6 7 8 9 10	1.771 561 0000 1.948 717 1000 2.143 588 8100 2.357 947 6910 2.593 742 4601	7.715 610 0000 9.487 171 0000 11.435 888 1000 13.579 476 9100 15.937 424 6010	.129 607 3804 .105 405 4997 .087 444 0176 .073 640 5391 .062 745 3949
	11 12 13 14 15	2.853 116 7061 3.138 428 3767 3.452 271 2144 3.797 498 3358 4.177 248 1694	18.531 167 0611 21.384 283 7672 24.522 712 1439 27.974 983 3583 31.772 481 6942	.053 963 1420 .046 763 3151 .040 778 5238 .035 746 2232 .031 473 7769
	16 17 18 19 20	4.594 972 9864 5.054 470 2850 5.559 917 3135 6.115 909 0448 6.727 499 9493	35.949 729 8636 40.544 702 8499 45.599 173 1349 51.159 090 4484 57.274 999 4933	.027 816 6207 .024 664 1344 .021 930 2222 .019 546 8682 .017 459 6248
ANNUALLY If compounded *annually* nominal annual rate is **10%**	21 22 23 24 25	7.400 249 9443 8.140 274 9387 8.954 302 4326 9.849 732 6758 10.834 705 9434	64.002 499 4426 71.402 749 3868 79.543 024 3255 88.497 326 7581 98.347 059 4339	.015 624 3898 .014 005 0630 .012 571 8127 .011 299 7764 .010 168 0722
SEMIANNUALLY If compounded *semiannually* nominal annual rate is **20%**	26 27 28 29 30	11.918 176 5377 13.109 994 1915 14.420 993 6106 15.863 092 9717 17.449 402 2689	109.181 765 3773 121.099 941 9150 134.209 936 1065 148.630 929 7171 164.494 022 6889	.009 159 0386 .008 257 6423 .007 451 0132 .006 728 0747 .006 079 2483
	31 32 33 34 35	19.194 342 4958 21.113 776 7454 23.225 154 4199 25.547 669 8619 28.102 436 8481	181.943 424 9578 201.137 767 4535 222.251 544 1989 245.476 698 6188 271.024 368 4806	.005 496 2140 .004 971 7167 .004 499 4063 .004 073 7064 .003 689 7051
QUARTERLY If compounded *quarterly* nominal annual rate is **40%**	36 37 38 39 40	30.912 680 5329 34.003 948 5862 37.404 343 4448 41.144 777 7893 45.259 255 5682	299.126 805 3287 330.039 485 8616 364.043 434 4477 401.447 777 8925 442.592 555 6818	.003 343 0638 .003 029 9405 .002 746 9250 .002 490 9840 .002 259 4144
	41 42 43 44 45	49.785 181 1250 54.763 699 2375 60.240 069 1612 66.264 076 0774 72.890 483 6851	487.851 811 2499 537.636 992 3749 592.400 691 6124 652.640 760 7737 718.904 836 8510	.002 049 8028 .001 859 9911 .001 688 0466 .001 532 2365 .001 391 0047
MONTHLY If compounded *monthly* nominal annual rate is **120%**	46 47 48 49 50	80.179 532 0536 88.197 485 2590 97.017 233 7849 106.718 957 1634 117.390 852 8797	791.795 320 5361 871.974 852 5897 960.172 337 8487 1057.189 571 6336 1163.908 528 7970	.001 262 9527 .001 146 8221 .001 041 4797 .000 945 9041 .000 859 1740
	51 52 53 54 55	129.129 938 1677 142.042 931 9844 156.247 225 1829 171.871 947 7012 189.059 142 4713	1281.299 381 6766 1410.429 319 8443 1552.472 251 8287 1708.719 477 0116 1880.591 424 7128	.000 780 4577 .000 709 0040 .000 644 1339 .000 585 2336 .000 531 7476
$i = .1$ $j_{(2)} = .2$ $j_{(4)} = .4$ $j_{(12)} = 1.2$	56 57 58 59 60	207.965 056 7184 228.761 562 3902 251.637 718 6293 276.801 490 4922 304.481 639 5414	2069.650 567 1841 2277.615 623 9025 2506.377 186 2927 2758.014 904 9220 3034.816 395 4142	.000 483 1734 .000 439 0556 .000 398 9822 .000 362 5796 .000 329 5092
	n	$s=(1+i)^n$	$s_{\overline{n}}=\dfrac{(1+i)^n-1}{i}$	$\dfrac{1}{s_{\overline{n}}}=\dfrac{i}{(1+i)^n-1}$

PRESENT WORTH OF 1 *What $1 due in the future is worth today.*	PRESENT WORTH OF 1 PER PERIOD *What $1 payable periodically is worth today.*	PARTIAL PAYMENT *Annuity worth $1 today.* *Periodic payment necessary to pay off a loan of $1.*	P E R I O D S	RATE **10%**
.909 090 9091	.909 090 9091	1.100 000 0000	1	
.826 446 2810	1.735 537 1901	.576 190 4762	2	
.751 314 8009	2.486 851 9910	.402 114 8036	3	.1
.683 013 4554	3.169 865 4463	.315 470 8037	4	
.620 921 3231	3.790 786 7694	.263 797 4808	5	*per period*
.564 473 9301	4.355 260 6995	.229 607 3804	6	
.513 158 1182	4.868 418 8177	.205 405 4997	7	
.466 507 3802	5.334 926 1979	.187 444 0176	8	
.424 097 6184	5.759 023 8163	.173 640 5391	9	
.385 543 2894	6.144 567 1057	.162 745 3949	10	
.350 493 8995	6.495 061 0052	.153 963 1420	11	
.318 630 8177	6.813 691 8229	.146 763 3151	12	
.289 664 3797	7.103 356 2026	.140 778 5238	13	
.263 331 2543	7.366 687 4569	.135 746 2232	14	
.239 392 0494	7.606 079 5063	.131 473 7769	15	
.217 629 1358	7.823 708 6421	.127 816 6207	16	
.197 844 6689	8.021 553 3110	.124 664 1344	17	
.179 858 7899	8.201 412 1009	.121 930 2222	18	
.163 507 9908	8.364 920 0917	.119 546 8682	19	
.148 643 6280	8.513 563 7198	.117 459 6248	20	
.135 130 5709	8.648 694 2907	.115 624 3898	21	ANNUALLY If compounded *annually* nominal annual rate is **10%**
.122 845 9736	8.771 540 2643	.114 005 0630	22	
.111 678 1578	8.883 218 4221	.112 571 8127	23	
.101 525 5980	8.984 744 0201	.111 299 7764	24	
.092 295 9982	9.077 040 0182	.110 168 0722	25	
.083 905 4529	9.160 945 4711	.109 159 0386	26	
.076 277 6844	9.237 223 1556	.108 257 6423	27	
.069 343 3495	9.306 566 5051	.107 451 0132	28	
.063 039 4086	9.369 605 9137	.106 728 0747	29	
.057 308 5533	9.426 914 4670	.106 079 2483	30	
.052 098 6848	9.479 013 1518	.105 496 2140	31	SEMIANNUALLY If compounded *semiannually* nominal annual rate is **20%**
.047 362 4407	9.526 375 5926	.104 971 7167	32	
.043 056 7643	9.569 432 3569	.104 499 4063	33	
.039 142 5130	9.608 574 8699	.104 073 7064	34	
.035 584 1027	9.644 158 9726	.103 689 7051	35	
.032 349 1843	9.676 508 1569	.103 343 0638	36	
.029 408 3494	9.705 916 5063	.103 029 9405	37	
.026 734 8631	9.732 651 3694	.102 746 9250	38	
.024 304 4210	9.756 955 7903	.102 490 9840	39	
.022 094 9282	9.779 050 7185	.102 259 4144	40	
.020 086 2983	9.799 137 0168	.102 049 8028	41	QUARTERLY If compounded *quarterly* nominal annual rate is **40%**
.018 260 2712	9.817 397 2880	.101 859 9911	42	
.016 600 2465	9.833 997 5345	.101 688 0466	43	
.015 091 1332	9.849 088 6678	.101 532 2365	44	
.013 719 2120	9.862 807 8798	.101 391 0047	45	
.012 472 0109	9.875 279 8907	.101 262 9527	46	
.011 338 1918	9.886 618 0825	.101 146 8221	47	
.010 307 4470	9.896 925 5295	.101 041 4797	48	
.009 370 4064	9.906 295 9359	.100 945 9041	49	
.008 518 5513	9.914 814 4872	.100 859 1740	50	
.007 744 1375	9.922 558 6247	.100 780 4577	51	MONTHLY If compounded *monthly* nominal annual rate **120%**
.007 040 1250	9.929 598 7498	.100 709 0040	52	
.006 400 1137	9.935 998 8634	.100 644 1339	53	
.005 818 2851	9.941 817 1486	.100 585 2336	54	
.005 289 3501	9.947 106 4987	.100 531 7476	55	
.004 808 5001	9.951 914 9988	.100 483 1734	56	
.004 371 3637	9.956 286 3626	.100 439 0556	57	
.003 973 9670	9.960 260 3296	.100 398 9822	58	$i = .1$
.003 612 6973	9.963 873 0269	.100 362 5796	59	$j_{(2)} = .2$ $j_{(4)} = .4$
.003 284 2703	9.967 157 2972	.100 329 5092	60	$j_{(12)} = 1.2$
$v^n = \dfrac{1}{(1+i)^n}$	$a_{\overline{n}\rceil} = \dfrac{1-v^n}{i}$	$\dfrac{1}{a_{\overline{n}\rceil}} = \dfrac{i}{1-v^n}$	n	

Index

About the Author

William Loscalzo, CPA, is vice president of Smith, Barney Real Estate Corporation. In this position he is responsible for the accounting and financial reporting of Security Capital Corporation, a public financial service holding company managed by a wholly owned subsidiary of Smith, Barney Real Estate Corporation. He is also a partner in Loscalzo Associates, a firm offering quality control and continuing professional education consulting services to the accounting profession. He is a member of the American Institute of Certified Public Accountants, the New York State Society of CPAs, and the New Jersey Society of CPAs. Mr. Loscalzo received a B.S. in accounting from Fordham University and an M.B.A. in taxation from Baruch College.